PERSONALITIES OF ANTIQUITY

PERSONALITIES
OF ANTIQUITY

BY

ARTHUR WEIGALL

Essay Index Reprint Series

BOOKS FOR LIBRARIES PRESS

FREEPORT, NEW YORK

First Published 1928
Reprinted 1969

STANDARD BOOK NUMBER:
8369-1217-9

LIBRARY OF CONGRESS CATALOG CARD NUMBER:
77-90672

PRINTED IN THE UNITED STATES OF AMERICA

FOREWORD

THE discovery of the tomb of Tutankhamen in November, 1922, did a great deal more than deliver a buried collection of unique and priceless works of art of the far past to the public gaze of the present day. It marked the beginning of a definite epoch in the mental life of the man in the street, for it opened his eyes to a region of romantic interest which had previously been hid from him by no more than the absence of the will to perceive it. Something happened to him when he read the news of the opening of the Pharaoh's sepulchre: he became aware suddenly and for the first time that the long researches of the historian, the philologist, and archæologist had extended the possible range of his interests far beyond their former scope, far beyond the province of his own experience or of the recorded experiences of his contemporaries. A new form of entertainment of infinite variety was presented to him; a new way of forgetting for a while the humdrum business of his daily life; a new means of accomplishing that flight from himself which is man's most inveterate occupation.

His changed attitude towards that marvellous Past which he had once so contemptuously ignored can best be demonstrated by recording its consequences upon my own work, though I am not at all sure that it is in the best taste to do so. Before the year of this great discovery, and while I was serving the Egyptian Government in the capacity of Inspector-General of Antiquities, I had published various books dealing in a more or less readable manner with matters of ancient history, but their sales had been limited to a single edition. Since 1922, volumes such as my *Life and Times of Akhnaton* and my *Life and Times of Cleopatra,* formerly little read, have passed through I know not how many editions. Previous to that year I had sometimes sent articles to the newspapers on similar subjects, but usually they had been returned to me as not being of general interest. In the last two years, however, I have been writing long courses of articles on history and archæology; and these have been read by hundreds of thousands of people.

My despatches from Egypt in the early spring of 1923 were printed in so many newspapers that they were daily read, I am told, by nearly a hundred million people, not more than a negligible fraction of which number would have troubled to read such matter at an earlier date. Previous to 1922 I delivered an occasional lecture, but it was only to a small audience of students: in 1923, however, I addressed, I suppose, well over a hundred thousand people in Great Britain and America, and the limit was only set by my laziness or lack of time. These personal experiences show so clearly the surprising change which has taken place that I will perhaps be pardoned for recording them here.

The man in the street has discovered Antiquity. In his flight from himself and from the ceaseless rat-tat of his driven brain, he has invaded the regions of the Past, previously believed to be very largely the private property of Professor Dryasdust. He used to scoff at that region as a place of bones, fenced about by a very stockade of unintelligible and impenetrable technicalities, but now he has seen suddenly that it lies open and alluring before him. He knows that he has only to step on to the magic carpet and make the flight across the centuries, in order to break out of the endless circle of his narrow experience, and to find himself a care-free spectator of scenes and events which are but the more enthralling because they belong to an age remote from his sometimes tedious to-day.

Actually, however, he has only penetrated as yet into certain areas of the new territory. Egypt at a particular period has occupied much of his attention; Rome in the days of the Empire has received his less protracted visits; the forgotten civilization of South America has been the goal of a brief journey. But now he needs to broaden the range of his interests so that he may discover how infinite is the extent of that vast Antiquity into which he has adventured; and since the widening of his travels in the far Past is all to the good, in that it serves to foster further research on the part of the actual workers in this great field, I have amused myself by calling to mind, more or less at random, some of the various subjects which have taken my own fancy, and have written a few pages about them as they occurred to me, telling myself that, since they had aroused my own extremely normal interest, they would certainly arouse other people's. At the round number of thirty such little studies I paused, having, indeed, no time to continue the process; and, reading over what I had written, it seemed to me that these thirty sketches might serve in some degree the purpose I had in mind, namely, that of extending the range of the general reader's travels in the huge field of Antiquity.

With this end in view, therefore, I have made a book of them: a trivial book, it is true, yet written out of a love of that romantic and far-off region which is not trivial, but is, indeed, to me the very salt of life.

CONTENTS

PERSONALITIES OF ANTIQUITY

I

ELAGABALUS, THE GOLDEN LUNATIC

THE character of Elagabalus, Emperor of Rome, is, on moral grounds, to be ranked as one of the most objectionable in ancient history. I want, however, to describe some of the amusements of his Court during the four years of his astonishing reign (A.D. 218–222), and this I cannot do without saying a word or two about the scandalous youth himself.

His real name was Varius Avitus Bassianus, but on coming to the throne he was called Marcus Aurelius Antoninus—the same names as those borne by Caracalla, his reputed father. Later he identified himself so closely with Elah-Gabal, the sun-god of Emesa in Syria, of whom his family supplied the hereditary High Priests, that he came to be known as Elagabalus or Heliogabalus. He was no more than fourteen years of age when the army proclaimed him Emperor; and he was only eighteen when he was murdered and dropped down the main drain of Rome.

He came of very mixed blood; but that, of course, hardly mattered in the metropolis which was then the great melting-pot of the nations, comparable in that respect with modern New York, a sort of extra-territorial area wherein the amiable assimilation of inimical breeds is to be observed in full swing. If it be true, as his mother stoutly maintained, that her illicit relations with the Emperor Caracalla had called him into existence, then Elagabalus must have been a mixture of Tripolitan (i.e., North-African) and Syrian; but if his legal father was his actual parent, as, of course, was possible even in the fashionable circles of the time, then he was Syrian on both sides.

Actually, the boy looked more like a German, for he had golden hair, large blue eyes, and a very fair skin; but his nature, nevertheless, was less western than eastern, and his shocking and precocious sensuousness was, we may hope, derived from some strain quite foreign to ourselves. Nobody could wish to claim racial kinship with this appalling youth, in spite of his undoubtedly great beauty; and it is a matter of satisfaction that his true origin will now never be known.

His extravagances were astonishing even to the Romans, and the sums of money spent upon his entertainments were so fabulous that the most apathetic millionaries of to-day would be shaken by them. His banquets entirely put into the shade those of the Inimitable Livers of two-and-a-half centuries earlier, which I shall describe in a subsequent chapter; and his expenditure in general was such that one may suppose him to have had little expectation of a long reign, it being his custom, indeed, to carry poison with him at all times, so that at the first clear signs of the end he might make a painless exit from the scenes of his revels.

Amongst the dishes prepared by his chefs I may record the following: peacocks' tongues flavoured with cinnamon; ostriches' and flamingoes' brains served with anchovy sauce; the brains of thrushes, parrots, and pheasants; spiders in aspic; sows' udders with truffles; dormice baked in poppies and honey; pigs served cold and whole, from which, when carved, live birds flew out, and hot sausages came tumbling after them; a salad consisting of mullets' fins and cress, flavoured with mint; sausages made of lampreys' roes, oysters and lobsters; and small fish served as though alive in a transparent sauce which looked like the blue Mediterranean.

Some of the dishes were prepared more with a view to their appeal to the sense of sight than to that of taste. Thus he would sprinkle the yellow peas with pellets of gold, or the lentils with rubies, or would cause lumps of clouded amber to be served with the brown beans: which must have been hard on the teeth of his more short-sighted guests. There were often as many as twenty-two courses to a meal; and the absurd and restless boy would sometimes insist that a certain dish required a certain setting, and would make the whole company rise and journey with him across the city to another palace or pavilion, only to find that they were to move on again to yet another place for the following course.

Being but a child, however, he liked thus to vent his whims, or even to play heavy pranks upon his friends. If one of them fell into a drunken sleep, for example, he might cause him to be carried to a room where, when he woke up, he would find himself shut in with two or three prowling tigers or leopards: the creatures were tame, of course, and their keepers were near at hand, but the victim did not know it, and, in one case, indeed, actually died of fright. Or he would seat a guest upon a concealed air-cushion which would suddenly be deflated just as the man was drinking his soup, or was engaged in some similarly delicate operation.

At other times he would have wax representations of game or other meat put before the diners to deceive them, or would powder the bread with crushed pearls instead of grain, or serve crystals in place of sweets. Yet again he would hold a competition and present the winner with a dead dog as a prize, although on the previous day he might have given a huge fortune to the successful competitor. Sometimes, too, he would cause an old hag or a hideous negress to slip into the place of some beautiful dancing-girl who had been reclining beside one of his drunken guests.

He was only a boy, it must always be remembered, and his jokes were such as might have been played by any imaginative child, who had been given unlimited power and fabulous wealth. He is said, however, to have presented rewards of enormous value to the victims of his pranks who had taken his fun in good part; and, indeed, so often did he give his guests all the plate used at the banquets they had attended that the goldsmiths, if not the Treasury, had difficulty in keeping pace with his generosity.

At public festivals, too, he flung money in cartloads to the people, distributing amongst them also oxen, camels, horses, carriages, slaves, clothes, stuffs, and gold and silver vases. At such popular displays the streets were strewn with yellow sand powdered over with glistening gold-dust, and roses, narcissus, violets, and lilies were tossed before him.

The spectacles in the amphitheatre with which he regaled the citizens might have been conceived by any slightly demented schoolboy. To the din of a brass band of over a thousand instruments, chariot-races were run in which the cars were drawn by lions, tigers, stags, and dogs; wild elephants were sent into the ring to battle with untamed lions; trained animals, their fur sprinkled with gold, were made to perform extraordinary and often very rude tricks; herds of ostriches were chased by comic hunters; and acrobats vaulted over the backs of wild zebras. At these entertainments he reclined in the royal box, his cheeks rouged and his eyelids darkened, his fingers weighed down with rings, and his effeminate arms encircled with bracelets, while beautiful slaves sprinkled perfumes over him or plied him with sweetmeats upon jewel-encrusted dishes of gold.

In hot weather he caused snow to be brought with infinite labour from the mountains to cool his drinks, and once he made his slaves work all night to erect a mound of snow in his private orchard, so that he might pelt his friends with snowballs for a few minutes on a summer's morning. On another occasion he obliged his court to drive chariots drawn by wild stags through the porticoes of the palace, the marble floors of which had been powdered with gold and silver dust; and once he himself took part in a race in which the jewel-studded chariots were drawn by fantastically caparisoned elephants and camels.

The ceremonies in honour of Elah-Gabal, whom he vainly attempted to raise to the position of sole god of Rome, were of the most extravagant character. Oxen and sheep were slaughtered by the thousand as sacrifices at lamp-lit altars heaped high with rare and heavily perfumed flowers; and libations of wine were poured out in red rivers over the alabaster floors. At these ceremonies the yellow-haired boy officiated as High Priest, arrayed in the most amazing robes ablaze with gold, a gold tiara on his head and top-boots of gilded leather on his feet; and the sight of him moving about in a cloud of incense, his face painted like a courtesan's, and his eyes heavy with drugs, was one which could never be forgotten. He looked, indeed, like a golden lunatic in the Bedlam of a dream.

At all times his clothes were extraordinary. He generally wore thin silk robes of purple or green, his favourite colours; and sometimes he appeared in cloth of gold sewn with precious stones. He was decked all over with blazing jewellery; and his dazzling shoes and sandals were the talk of Rome. On some occasions his and his guests' garments were by arrangement all of one colour, and the furniture and every dish set before them was of the same hue.

The rooms of his palace had walls of rare marbles inlaid with precious stones, and in some cases there were ivory ceilings from which carved flowers hung down. One hall was built with a dome of sapphire, a floor of malachite, crystal columns, and red-gold walls. The couches on which his friends reclined at his banquets were made of solid silver, with coverings of hare's fur or partridge's down, and with cushions of purple and gold. On these occasions everybody was souced with rare scents, and saffron mixed with gold-dust was sprinkled in showers over them.

The use of perfumes was profuse. Even the wine was scented or spiced, sometimes pine cones being introduced, and sometimes cinnamon, myrrh, or crushed roses. Drugs, too, were added; and a certain mixture of white wine, absinthe, honey, roses and strong-smelling spikenard, was much in favour, while sleep-bringing poppies were largely used.

Scents, wines, foods, and all else, were valued by him according to their rarity and costliness; and the waste of money was in itself a cause of pleasurable excitement to him. His very dogs, people said, were fed on foie-gras, his horses on rare grapes, and his tame leopards on pheasants and parroquets.

At last there came the time when his subjects grew tired of the excesses of this half-demented youth, so they murdered him one day, before he had time to take his own life. He left behind him a memory nauseating in most respects to decent Romans; but there was one good thing to be said about him, namely, that he hated to see people unhappy, and did his best, after his own lights, to keep himself and everybody about him in an endless and blissful dream. Nevertheless, the sewer into which his body was dropped was probably the most appropriate place for him.

II

THE QUEEN OF SHEBA

AFTER the defeat and suicide of King Theodore of
Abyssinia and the sack of Magdala in 1868, the British
Army brought back to England numerous Ethiopic
manuscripts, which were placed in the British Museum.
Amongst these there were two copies of the Kebra
Nagast or "Glory of the Kings," an ancient work much
venerated in Abyssinia as containing the proofs that
the royal house of that country was descended from
King Solomon and the Queen of Sheba; and in 1872
the negro King John IV wrote to the British Government asking that this book might be returned to him
because his people would not obey him without it. The
Trustees of the British Museum, therefore, sent back one
of the two copies; but the other, which dated from
about 1320 and was obviously an Ethiopic translation
of a much earlier work, was kept in London, and an
English rendering of it, made by Sir E. A. Wallis
Budge, was published a few years ago.

From the Kebra Nagast, as well as from the Bible,
the Korân, and legends still current in Abyssinia and
Arabia, one may gather some of the traditions regarding

the Queen of Sheba, who was undoubtedly an historic character, living about the year 1000 B.C.; and it may be of interest here to piece these tales together into some sort of narrative.

The Queen, who is called Mâkeda in the Kebra Nagast, and Balkîs in the Korân, ruled the country of the Sabaeans, the inhabitants of Southern Arabia, her capital being in the neighbourhood of Sana, some two hundred miles north of Aden, and her dominions extending across the narrow Straits of Bab el-Mandeb to the shores of East Africa. She was probably a woman of Arabian blood, rather than the negress her connection with Abyssinia would suggest; and she is said to have been clever and beautiful, though she had one unfortunate defect, namely, that her legs were far too hairy to be pretty, at least, that is what some of the traditions say, though others state that the defect was a localized patch of hair on the heel of one foot.

She was descended from a dynasty of five Sabaean Kings whose names, according to a manuscript now at Oxford, were Arâwi, Angâbo, Giedur, Siebado, and Kawnâsya. Her kingdom, however, though wealthy and prosperous, was remote from the great centres of civilization, and would hardly have been known to the peoples of the east end of the Mediterranean had it not been for the fact that the sailors and merchants of these countries sometimes made journeys down the Red Sea to obtain gold, and also to buy the fragrant gums of the south with which to make incense and perfumes. By this means stories of the wealth of the Sabaeans had reached the ears of Solomon, whose kingdom had recently risen to considerable importance, and whose luxurious court at Jerusalem was much talked about in the neighbouring countries; and, similarly, accounts of Solomon's riches and personal attractiveness had reached the Queen of Sheba.

At length the Jewish King, desiring to obtain a monopoly of the gold and gums of this southern land, despatched messengers to the Queen, ordering her to give special facilities to his traders; whereupon she sent him a pacificatory present of slaves, gold, precious stones, and gums, although her people had advised her to return a more dignified and less conciliatory answer. Solomon, however, treated her embassy with disdain, and at this the Queen decided to go herself to Jerusalem, being urged to do so, also, by the exciting stories she had heard of his magnificence and his personal charm.

She therefore set out in great state, with a caravan consisting of nearly eight hundred camels and innumerable donkeys, bearing a huge treasure of gold, precious stones, and spices and gums. The journey from her capital to Solomon's, by the caravan-route along the Arabian coast of the Red Sea, was some 1400 miles in length; and it must have taken her three months or more to accomplish it. But at length, she reached her destination, and her arrival was regarded as one of the most noteworthy events in all that short-lived period of Jewish national grandeur.

Solomon was delighted with her, and she with him. He found her exceedingly attractive, and she, on her part, was deeply impressed by his intelligence and his handsome appearance. He spent a great deal of time in her company, telling her about the great world of which she knew very little; and since his voice was musical and sympathetic, and his figure superb, she was pleased to allow him to entertain her in this manner for hours on end, and, at last, fell head over ears in love with him. One day, however, she had to cross a court-yard of the palace which had been flooded—I suppose by a recent rain-storm, though people said that Solomon had done it on purpose; and having lifted up her skirts she inadvertently exposed her ugly defect, whereupon the King, after one glance, hastily sent his best doctors to her, who, by using a depilatory, the secret of which is now unfortunately lost, soon had her cured.

At length the King, according to his invariable habit, suggested that she should become his wife, which, in view of the fact that, as she admitted, the half had not been told her about him, was no very flattering offer; and it is not surprising to hear that at first she refused him. Nevertheless, a woman cannot easily re-sist the temptation to cut out another woman who has attracted the man she loves, and, in the case of the

Queen of Sheba, the thought of cutting out seven hundred wives and three hundred concubines must have been quite irresistible.

At any rate, she wandered one night into his bedroom on the pretext of looking for a glass of water to drink; and the sequel, being not otherwise than that which was to be expected, need not be recorded. I have only to add that the story as related by tradition runs thus: Solomon had entertained her that evening to a supper of ten courses of highly seasoned and strongly salted food, and afterwards had caused every drop of water to be removed from every jug or drinking-vessel in the place, except from the carafe which stood at his own bedside. In the night, of course, she was parched with thirst, and therefore roamed about in search of something to drink, and thus quite accidentally found herself in his room. That, I take it, was *her* story.

A few weeks later, when their mutual ardour had cooled, she returned to her own country, loaded with gifts, amongst which was the King's ring, given to her in lieu of marriage lines; and in due course she became the mother of a fine boy, to whom she gave the names of David and Menyelek, generally calling him, however, Bayna-Lehkem, "the son of the wise man."

When this boy had grown to manhood, she told him the secret of his parentage, whereupon he insisted upon going to Jerusalem to make his father's acquaintance.

The Queen, therefore, gave him a letter of introduction to Solomon, and also the royal ring; but there was no need to show either of these to the King: everybody in Jerusalem recognized him at once, for he was the image of his father.

Up to this point the stories, on the whole, are plausible enough, and there is no need to discard them as unhistorical simply because they have no contemporary confirmation. But now comes an incident which is so obviously intended to enhance the glory of Abyssinia that one has to look at it with incredulity. The Queen and her people had been worshippers of the sun, moon, and stars; but now the superiority of Jehovah over the ancestral gods was apparent, and there was a general desire amongst the Sabaeans to have in their own country some object from the Jewish Temple which they might venerate. The young prince, being nothing if not thorough, is said, therefore, to have stolen the Ark of the Lord from the Holy of Holies in Jerusalem, substituting a facsimile in its place, and to have carried it back to his own land, whence it was taken at length across the straits to Abyssinia. Thus, Zion, the seat of Jehovah, was transferred to the south; and for ever afterwards the Kings of Abyssinia, the descendants of the Sabaeans, have been the guardians of the real and only home of the True God, and shall continue to be so until the Second Coming.

"Thus we know," says the Kebra Nagast, "that of a

surety the King of Ethiopia is King of Zion and the first-born seed of Shem, and that God loveth exceedingly the people of Ethiopia, and hath made for the Kings of Ethiopia more glory and grace and majesty than for all the other Kings of the earth."

III

A LITTLE SCANDAL ABOUT JULIUS CÆSAR

THE question is, has Julius Cæsar been dead long enough for us to rake up with impunity some of the old scandal about him, or ought we to make our bow to the altar of the god of Oblivion and leave the shocking gossip hid in the darkness of the ages yet a while longer? After all, it is not so very long ago that he was riding down the lanes of Kent, Middlesex, and Hertford, making friends or enemies of our British forefathers: it is only a matter of some two thousand years since then, a figure which represents no more than sixty generations.

Still, there is a certain intellectual amusement to be derived from scandal which can no longer hurt the personal feelings of any living man; and, indeed, in the case of the gossip about Cæsar there is a moral to be extracted from it which will be apparent to anyone who will make with me the flight across the centuries to the houses of the scandalmongers of ancient Rome.

When I look around me in modern cities such as London, and see on all sides those pale-faced and elegant young men who emulate the manners of women, I do not give way to utter despair, but say rather to myself that even so was the great Julius Cæsar at the outset of his career. It is true that in later years he merely exchanged this effeminacy for a libertinism which earned for him the reputation of being the inevitable co-respondent in every fashionable divorce; but the moral is not wholly extinguished by the fact, for he found time to create and govern an empire and to become a shining instance of the superman. The lesson, therefore, is that there is still hope for the temporarily emasculated.

As a young man Julius Cæsar was remarkably handsome, and, having been taken up by a number of artistic and fashionable youths whom it was considered rather smart to know, he began to spend a great deal of time and thought upon his personal appearance. He used to have himself carefully scented after his bath, and he made the barber put a nice wave into his hair with the tongs. Soon he added a little rouge to his cheeks, and a touch of red on his lips; and I take it that he powdered his nose.

One of the leaders of this set was the good-looking Nicomedes, King of Bithynia, the region just east of Constantinople on the shores of the Black Sea; and the young Cæsar, having gone to stay with him in his own country, was jestingly called the Queen of Bithynia by the Roman wags. Another of Cæsar's intimate friends was Pompey, who, by reason of his elegance, was nicknamed King of Rome; and thus Cæsar himself came to be termed Queen of Rome, a designation which caused loud laughter amongst those whom it did not nauseate.

Then came a sudden change. The young man had far too much common sense to believe for long that his artistic and intellectual tastes were only to be served by this precious group; and soon we find him distinguishing himself in other fields. He was a clever swordsman, a powerful swimmer, a fine athlete, and a perfect horseman; and a certain passion for adventure and excitement led him at length to take up soldiering with enthusiasm, and already at the age of twenty-one he had won the civic crown by very bravely saving a soldier's life at the storming of Mytilene.

Thereupon he stopped waving his hair and rouging his cheeks, and allowed himself full use of the opportunities for romantic intrigues which came his way by reason of the sheer adoration he now inspired in women. The ladies went mad about him; he was so handsome—beautiful in fact, so brave, so dashing, so well-dressed, so clever, so artistic; and he had an understanding way with women utterly denied to the rough, "caveman" type of youth which was the usual alternative to the effeminate kind.

Of course there were things to be said against him in his new heroic rôle. His voice was rather high and shrill; his skin, as Plutarch says, was very soft and white; his walk, it seems, was odd, being perhaps of that somewhat mincing variety peculiar to the clique he had abandoned; and he had the now much burlesqued habit of running his fingers delicately through his hair. His manner of speech, too, was affected; and, fancying himself as a poet, he used to read his own verses to his friends in rather a boring manner.

Nevertheless, there can be no question that he was very charming; and his manner of life had just that exotic character which women liked. He was not very rich, but he lived in such magnificence that at an early age he was up to his eyes in debt, yet shouldered his burden of some £280,000 or $1,400,000 with the utmost levity. Once, when he was still young, he was captured by pirates, who demanded a ransom of twenty talents (about £5000 or $25,000); but he pretended to be very insulted at this, declaring that he was worth at least fifty, and he sent off his attendants to procure that sum for his release.

He had to wait over a month for the arrival of the money, and during that time he treated his bloodthirsty captors with the most reckless insolence. If he wished to sleep, and they were making a noise, he would order them to be quiet; and, slapping them jovially on the back, he would tell them that he would have them all crucified one day. He "ragged" them, joined in their races and games, jeered at them when he defeated them, insisted on them listening to his verses round the camp fire, calling them illiterate fools when they did not applaud, and generally carried himself with such extraordinary indifference to his danger, that he aroused their hearty admiration.

I may add that as soon as he was released, he manned a ship, and attacked and captured the whole band, whereupon, just as he had warned them, he caused them all to be crucified. The story was the talk of Rome.

His marriages were a disgrace. First he married Cossutia, solely for the sake of her money. Then he fell in love with Cornelia, divorced his first wife, and married her. She did not live long, and very soon after her death he married Pompeia for purely political reasons. Next, he divorced her, and married Calpurnia; and she, too, he tried to divorce, but afterwards abandoned the project. In later life he went off with Cleopatra, and with Eunoe, Queen of Mauretania; but, returning to Cleopatra, he was for the second time about to divorce Calpurnia so that he might marry the Egyptian Queen when he was murdered.

The marvel is that he did not end his life earlier, as Oman remarks, with a dagger between his ribs; for he was constantly infuriating husbands and lovers by having wild affairs with their wives or mistresses, and he was even unscrupulous enough to make a victim of Mucia, the wife of his best friend, Pompey. So notorious were his habits in this regard that in later years when he returned from the wars in Gaul, although he was then no longer young, and his looks were not

what they had been now that he had lost his hair, his
soldiers set everybody laughing by singing a rollicking
song, the refrain of which was *Urbani, servate
uxores!—calvum moechum adducimus,* which has the
meaning that the citizens should lock their wives up,
because the army was bringing back to Rome that baldheaded old sinner who was sure to be after them soon.

In warfare he was terrible, and the gossips estimated
that in Gaul alone he had killed a million men, and
had sent another million into slavery. People were very
angry with him about an attack he had made upon the
disarmed tribes of the Usipetes and Tencteri, whom he
massacred to a man after making peace with them; and
Cato went so far as to propose that he should be arrested
and sent in chains to the representatives of the
slaughtered people that they might wreak their vengeance upon him.

Yet sometimes his mercilessness was regarded as
rather amusing, as, for example, when he crucified the
pirates, as related above; and the story was told with
relish how once he had threatened instant death to a
certain Metellus who had disobeyed him, and had said
to him ". . . and you know, young man, this is more
disagreeable for me to threaten than to do."

But, after all, this is only scandal; and the splendid
features of Cæsar's character, and his many good deeds,
are altogether too apparent for us to be turned against
him by the tittle-tattle of Rome, even though we may

be certain, in his case, that where there was smoke there must have been fire. He was adored by his soldiers, who never tired of telling tales of his bravery, his generosity, his kindness, and his ability to share with them their hardships. All his life he inspired devotion in men as well as in women; and in the end his murderers were so hated that every one of them was hounded off the face of the earth.

De mortuis nil nisi bonum! Well, perhaps the greatest good one can say of the dead Cæsar is said by the record of these scandals; for they show how infinitely far the best that was in him rose above the sins and the weaknesses which caused his character so often to be adversely criticized when he was alive.

IV

THE BOLSHEVIKS OF 2200 *B. C.*

WHEN the downtrodden lower classes in France revolted against the aristocratic order in the year 1789,
members of the old nobility thought that the end of
the world had come, and many of them went to their
deaths with the fortifying consolation that no part of
the human race would long survive them. It was the
end, they supposed, and soon the executioners would
lie dead beside their victims, blasted by the last trump.
Yet the nightmare passed, and now it is but a memory
in the mind of diuturnal man.

In Russia, too, the great Bolshevik revolution was
regarded by many of its victims as the last act of the
world's drama. Mankind was about to perish; God had
withdrawn Himself; and death, even before a firing-
party, was a happy exit from an agonizing scene of
final chaos. Yet the high hour of terror passed, and the
process of adjustment to new conditions began, which,
in the end, will inevitably relegate the cataclysm to the
frontiers of Oblivion.

These things happen: there is nothing new under the
sun. Come with me to Egypt in about the year 2200

B.C., and look at the first recorded Bolshevik revolution. It was in many respects very similar to that which has recently taken place in Russia; and, terrible as it was, it passed, leaving behind it a memory which gradually faded into nothingness. Man's essential common sense and common humanity prevailed in the end; and there would have been no record of the upheaval available at all, had not a certain contemporary writer named Ipuwer committed his impressions to paper, and had not that document been dug up not many years ago from the sands of Egypt.

The intellectual but short-lived Ninth Dynasty (2271-2222 B.C.), which consisted of four Pharaohs of the name of Akhtoi, who had reigned over Middle and Lower Egypt, had recently come to an end; and now this northern part of the Nile Valley had fallen upon evil days, and the upstart War Lords who form the Tenth Dynasty had for five-and-twenty years fought with one another until their resources were exhausted, and nothing resembling stable government remained. Far up in the south a line of provincial kings, now known as the Eleventh Dynasty, had risen into power, and from their somewhat uncouth capital at Luxor were ruling all Upper Egypt with a rough, strong hand; and the very refined but now distracted citizens of the north must have cast many an envious glance towards these peaceful and prosperous southern realms, uncultured though they might be.

Then came the uprising of the Proletariat in the territory of the Tenth Dynasty, and the consequent Reign of Terror, which lasted until the southern monarch invaded the country, swept it clean, and made himself Pharaoh of the whole land; but it is about the events immediately preceding this salutary invasion that Ipuwer writes, addressing himself to the exiled representative of the northern throne, and imploring him to exert such power as is left to him both to stem the growing tide of communist revolution and to save the kingdom from the menace of invasion from the barbarous though well-organized upper country.

Ipuwer points out that the revolution is partly due to Semitic influence: at least he says that there are such swarms of aliens in Egypt, who have drifted in from the region of the later Palestine, and have become "Egyptians," that now there are no real Egyptians of any standing left. As a matter of fact, communist ideas are quite likely to have been propagated to some extent by these aliens, for the Semitic peoples of Syria, Palestine, and the deserts adjacent to Egypt, largely belonged to communities of municipalities of a more or less republican kind.

Ipuwer states the nature of the revolution in a few terse words. "Men have dared to rebel· against the Crown," he writes, "and a few lawless men have attempted to rid the land of its monarchy. The old order has perished. The Palace has been overthrown in a

minute. The King has been turned out by the Proletariat, and the treasury is the communal property of
everybody."

As a result of this upheaval a condition of things
had arisen with which we to-day are so familiar that
we can calmly weigh its advantages and disadvantages,
but which, to the writer of the ancient document before
us, was horrifying in the extreme.

"He who possessed no property," he gasps, "is now
a man of wealth. The poor of the land have become
rich, and the owners of property now have nothing.
He who was once a mere messenger himself, now gives
orders to messengers. Servants have given up perform-
ing the missions of their masters on which they were
sent, and are not afraid to do so. All women-servants
have become free with their tongues, and when their
mistresses speak to them they resent it. Gold and
precious stones adorn the necks of these female servants,
and though good things are in the land, the mistresses
of houses say: 'Would that we had something to eat!'—
for the poor have become the owners of the good
things."

"The possessors of fine clothes are now in rags," he
goes on. "He who had no bread is now owner of a barn,
and his cupboards are filled with other people's goods.
She who used to look at her face in the water is now
the possessor of a mirror. The wealthy are in mourning;
the once poor man rejoices. The son of a man of rank

is no longer distinguished from him who has no such father, for the families of the nobility have been thrust into the streets. Princes are starving in distress; noble ladies go hungry, and their bodies are in sad plight by reason of their rags."

"There have been terrible scenes," says Ipuwer. "The children of noble families have been dashed against the walls. The law-books of the Courts of Justice have been thrown out, and men have trodden on them in the public places. Government Offices have been rifled, and the income-tax lists have been carried off. Officials have been murdered, and their papers have been taken away. All is in ruins. Every city says: 'Let us suppress those in authority amongst us'; and though Right exists throughout the land in name, yet what men do, in appealing to it, is Wrong."

As a result of the revolution the state of the country is appalling, and life is cheap. "People's faces are pale," he writes, "for the criminal is at large, nor is there a man of yesterday left in authority. The peasant goes out to plough with his weapons in hand. Servants say 'Let's go and steal something.' A man looks upon his son as his enemy, and fights with his brother, or is killed at his brother's side. Men's hearts are violent. There is blood everywhere, nor is Death short of victims. No skilled labourers are working; for these enemies of their country have ruined its crafts. Moreover, sickness rages throughout the land."

There is, of course, a shortage of food and fuel. "The corn crops have perished on every side. No one ploughs his land. The cattle are left to stray, and there is none to shepherd the flocks. Men eat grass and wash it down with water. No food is found even for the birds. Gates, posts, and fences are used for fuel: boxes of expensive ebony, even, are smashed in pieces, and precious acacia-wood is chopped up for firewood. Squalor is apparent throughout the land, and there is none whose clothes are clean in these times."

"Pedestrians on the roads have to be guarded," he says, "for men lurk behind the bushes until the traveller comes along, so that they may rob him of his baggage, and take whatever is upon him. He is belaboured with the blows of their sticks, or barbarously murdered."

The religious life of the people, of course, has been destroyed, and a man's answer to any enquiry in this regard is "If I knew where God is, then I would make my prayers to Him." "There is no end of noise everywhere," Ipuwer writes, "but laughter has ceased, and it is groaning mingled with tears that fills the land. Old and young cry 'Would that I might die!'—and little children exclaim: 'My parents ought never to have caused me to live.' "

Ipuwer begs the fallen king to take courage and to attempt to restore order, imploring him to turn to God in this great catastrophe, and to pray for divine aid. Then, in a strangely significant and beautiful passage, he declares his belief that a Saviour will come, who "shall bring peace to that which is now fevered." He reminds the King of the prophecy which speaks of the advent some day of this Saviour, and says of Him that "He shall be the Shepherd of His people, and in Him shall there be no sin: when His flocks are scattered He shall spend the day in gathering them together."

Thus, in the firm belief that the goodness of human nature will in the end prevail, and that peace on earth will eventually return, he ends this remarkable document; and presently history has to record the establishment of law and order once more. The Terror passes, as do all such horrors, and soon the upheaval is utterly forgotten. These things happen; and maybe it is for the ultimate good of mankind that they do.

V

THE BEAR-KEEPER'S DAUGHTER

SOMEWHERE about the year A.D. 500 there lived at Constantinople a man named Acacius, whose business it was to feed and look after the bears which were baited and hunted at the big public circus. At that time the inhabitants of the great metropolis of the Eastern Roman Empire were split into two political factions, known as the Greens and the Blues, these having been originally sporting distinctions; and so bitter was the enmity between these parties that there could be no sharing of property in the circus or anywhere else, the result being that two sets of animals had to be kept for their bloodthirsty entertainments.

Acacius was in charge of the bears belonging to the Greens, and when suddenly he died his widow married the man who had been given his post; but this personage proved incompetent and was quickly dismissed, thus leaving the woman stranded with the three little daughters of her first marriage, whose names were Comito, Theodora, and Anastasia. These children were sent to the circus by their mother in an attempt to soften the heart of the manager for the Greens, the idea being, I suppose, that they should follow him about, crying and looking hungry; but the man would not take any notice of them. The manager for the Blues, however, happened to be on the premises, and he, very kindly, took the dismissed bear-keeper into his employment, whereupon the whole household abjured the Greens and all their works, and became staunch partisans of the Blues.

The family fortunes, however, were not what they had been in the lifetime of Acacius; and as soon as the eldest girl, Comito, was old enough to attract attention she was made to go on the stage, and very soon she had become the disreputable favourite of the theatrical and circus underworld. Her sister Theodora, who was still too young to follow in her footsteps, used to hang about the theatre most of the time; but a year or two later she also found employment on the stage, and was soon involved in all the horrors of that life, which, in those days, was one of the lowest of the low.

Theodora was a delicate child, with refined features and serious dark eyes; but there was something mis-chievous and impudent about her which quickly brought her success as a comic character in the rough burlesque and farces wherein she played a part. People remembered her afterwards as an impish little creature on the stage, who used to blow out her cheeks for the actors to slap, and who played the fool in these com-edies with a precocious sort of shamelessness which was thought to be very droll.

She never could learn to dance conventionally, however, and she had no voice for singing; but as time
passed her developing beauty and her great sense of fun
won her much fame, and soon she had supplanted her
elder sister as queen of this particular underworld. Men
fell in love with her, and she was often to be seen going out to supper with eight or ten of them at a time.
She seemed to have no morals whatsoever, and long before she was fully grown she had the reputation of
being the most dissolute little sinner in all Constantinople.

In figure she was now graceful though rather under-
sized. Her face was beautiful but deadly pale, and one
could see that she was not strong; yet her eyes, with
their solemn, intense expression, were full of fire, and
from time to time when she ceased for a while her jok-
ing she showed signs of deep and brooding thought and
of an increasing sensibility, marked by an audacious
contempt for the men whose chattel she was forced
to be.

At the age of eighteen or so she became the mother
of a daughter whose father is unknown to history; and
this sobered her to some extent, causing her heartily to
wish herself rid of the objectionable crowd with whom
she mixed. There then came into her life a certain
nobleman named Hecebolus who had just been appointed Governor of Pentapolis in North Africa; and
when he invited her to come with him to his new prov-

ince she readily accepted, and, having placed her little girl with foster-parents, she took ship across the Mediterranean in high hopes of a happier existence.

Hecebolus, however, proved to be just as unpleasant as her other male friends, and, after a violent quarrel with him, she decided to abandon altogether the loose life she had been leading, and in utter disgust sailed for Alexandria, the Egyptian capital, intent on finding work. Thence she drifted back to Constantinople once more, supporting herself now by spinning and dressmaking.

Here she was seen one day by Justinian, the middleaged nephew and heir of the reigning Emperor Justin, who knew something of her past history, and was enthralled both by her beauty and by the strength of character she had displayed in abandoning her former life. He was, in fact, the first decent man she had ever met, and her liking for him was immediate. Soon he was head over ears in love with her, and astonished her by asking her to be his wife; but their romance was thwarted by the action of Justinian's aunt Euphemia who pointed out that there was an old law which forbade any man of Senatorial rank to marry a woman who had been on the stage.

A year or so later, however, in 523, Euphemia died, and thereupon Justinian managed to have the law repealed, and at once married Theodora. It was not long before the old Emperor, likewise, died; and thus, almost at a bound, the little dressmaker and ex-courtesan, daughter of a common bear-keeper, found herself at the age of about two-and-twenty Empress of the East and the richest and most powerful woman in the world.

At first she lived as it were in a dream, and the luxuries of the marvellous palace seem to have held her in a state of ecstasy. She spent hours in her bath; she ate far too much at the banquets; and she fell off to sleep at all times of the day upon the enticing cushions of the rich divans. She made her husband take her to stay in all his palaces, and she kept going back to the one she liked best, which was situated at Hêrion, on the beautiful peninsula now called Phanaraki, on the shores of the Black Sea.

But soon she began to feel her power, and it was not long before the court realized that she had a driving-force more to be reckoned with than that of her husband. Justinian was a nervous type of man who could never sit still even at meals, but ate his food in snatches, hardly slept at all, and wandered about the palace at dead of night. He was a red-faced fellow, rather inclined to fatness; affable to all, but, so people said, not far to be trusted as a friend; much given to metaphysical speculations about the nature of God, but too callous to be a good Christian; self-willed and headstrong, but at times a bit of a coward. He adored his wife, however, and was ready enough to take her advice in state affairs, and to allow her to pursue her own course even when it was opposed to his own, as, for instance, in regard to the factions of the Greens and the Blues, she always having a dislike for the former, who had done her father a bad turn, while he, on the other hand, opposed the latter.

The memory of her experiences as a girl greatly influenced her actions as Empress. Naturally enough, she thought very ill of men in general, and was always interfering in domestic squabbles to defend wives against their husbands, even when the women had been faithless and the men justly incensed. Once when a certain young man spread the story that his bride had not been all that she should have been before her marriage, she had him turned up and spanked like a schoolboy for his slander. She conceived an intense hatred of vice in all its forms; and she astonished Constantinople by rounding up five hundred ladies of no reputation and packing them off to a palace across the Bosphorus, which she called the House of Repentance.

She attacked a certain high official at court named Priscus, whose ill-living had angered her, and when her husband defended him she had the man kidnapped and shipped off to the monastery at Cyzicus, where he was forcibly turned into a monk, the Emperor laughingly acquiescing when the audacious thing was done. She caused a law to be passed stopping what would now be

called the white slave traffic, and with her own money
she bought the freedom of hundreds of young girls shut
up in houses of ill-fame.

She put an end to the so-called sports at the circus
in which wild animals were hunted and slaughtered for
men's amusement; and she deliberately kept the greatest
nobles in the land waiting for an audience with her,
so that the stuffy little anteroom to her apartments was
always full of exasperated gentlemen ignominiously
standing on tip-toe in the hope that they would be
noticed by the ushers and admitted to her presence.

In this manner she exacted vengeance upon the other
sex for the disgraces of her childhood, though, to be
sure, there had been a time when she had played her
part in that squalid life with notorious zest; and, as her
power and influence increased, she took the greater
pleasure in humbling masculine pride. She introduced
a new court etiquette which obliged all men to prostrate
themselves before her—the whilom guttersnipe—when
they entered her presence; she caused officials to take the
oath of allegiance to her as well as to the Emperor; she
corresponded directly with foreign ambassadors in her
husband's absence, over the heads of the senators; and
in the Emperor's proclamations it was often stated that
he was acting on the advice of his beloved queen.

Then came the terrible Nika insurrection in the year
532, when the palace was besieged by the rebels, the city
was in flames, and death stared the imperial couple in

the face. All seemed to be lost, and Justinian, thoroughly scared, proposed that they should attempt to make their escape by ship across the Bosphorus. It was at this crisis that the greatness of Theodora's character displayed itself, for, turning contemptuously to the group of frightened men, she asked them why they should be afraid to die, since death must come at some time to all.

"For one who has reigned," she declared, "it would be intolerable to be an exile. May I never live to see the day on which those who meet me shall not call me Empress! If you wish to save yourselves, do so; there is no difficulty, for you have ample funds. There is the sea; there are the ships. But, for my own part, I abide by the old saying that 'Empire is a fair winding-sheet.' "

Under the lash of her tongue they rallied, and a successful sortie by the household troops quelled the rebellion. The rest of Justinian's reign was untroubled at home; but Theodora, never of very strong constitution, died in the year 547 at a comparatively early age, having lived long enough, however, to see the imperial capital rise to its greatest glory, and to witness the completion of the mighty cathedral of St. Sophia. Her memory has been much reviled by the contemporary writer Procopius, and by later historians; but if we make the flight across the centuries to the Constantinople of her day I think we shall find that the estimate of her character which I have here essayed is not far from the truth.

VI

THE KINDEST RACE OF THE ANCIENT WORLD

THERE are certain curious types of human nature which take an inordinate interest in the cruelties of the ancient world, and derive a concealed entertainment from reading descriptions of them or seeing them represented through some medium such as the cinema; and, indeed, so apparent is this strange taste that the film-producers of California and elsewhere, quick to exploit any means of appealing to all sorts and conditions, have been showing us for some years past the most disgusting representations of ancient bestiality of this kind.

On the stage, too, the same objectionable exhibitions have been placed before us, as in the case of the much-overrated play "Hassan," produced in London a few years ago, wherein a torture-scene was introduced which was beamed upon by critics who ought rather to have signified their disapproval in no hesitant voice, if only as a protest against the besmirching of the character of a great historical ruler, beloved of the friendly Persian nation.

In my opinion cruelty is a deadly sin, at once nauseating and infuriating to hear about or to see. I find in my own objection to it my nearest approach to the crank and the milksop; and it constitutes for me the chief blight upon the romance of Antiquity, for there can be no hiding the fact that in many lands and amongst many peoples cruelty was rampant in ancient times, and, indeed, it may be said that we are only now beginning to emerge from the age of inhumanity.

On all sides, it is true, there are still appalling instances of brutality to be noticed, either in regard to human beings or to animals; yet there are evident signs of a general awakening of the sensibilities, and it is distressing therefore to find those very cruelties of history which we are trying to live down, served up to us in the picture-house and the theatre for the entertainment of what must surely be a small and ever diminishing minority.

It may be argued that the producers of these spectacles are endeavouring to represent the truth, and that the truth must always be worth having; but in reply to this I would urge that such scenes, then, should only be introduced in connection with those nations which are actually known to have been cruel. The Romans, for example, were extremely brutal in the later periods of their history and the Assyrians were sometimes fiends incarnate; but certain other peoples were not thus tainted.

The kindest race of the ancient world was that of the Egyptians, and if we direct our course to the Nile

Valley of three or four thousand years ago, we shall find conditions there so humane that instances of Pharaonic cruelty such as we have been shown in some recent film-dramas will be seen at once to reflect the mentality of the producer and not that of the people he has thought to portray. The Egyptians were seldom consciously cruel: they did not grind men to pulp under the wheels of their juggernauts, they did not lash their labouring slaves, they did not torture people, they did not callously inflict death upon anybody—in fact they never did any of the things of this sort which the film-producers are at such pains to present to us.

Were we to find ourselves suddenly transported to the Egypt of the Pharaohs, we should soon see that there were two main causes of the remarkable absence of cruelty in this engaging people. Firstly, being by nature mild and kindly, the inhabitants of each town had early conceived of their particular deity as being a personification of benevolence; and hence they had assumed that they would have little chance of reaching heaven unless they could declare at their souls' judgment that they had committed no act of cruelty. A formal declaration of a clean sheet in this respect had at length come to be part of a man's religious obligation, and in the belief that "a man's conscience is the god within him," as they thoughtfully put it, every Egyptian had to endeavour to state that "his conscience was satisfied with his actions."

"I have committed no sin against my fellow-men," he had to declare; "I allowed no one to hunger; I caused no one to weep; I neither ordered murder nor committed it; I did not rob anybody; I did not make people afraid of me; I was not violent; I was not cruel, I gave bread to the hungry, water to the thirsty, and clothing to the naked." These things, and much more, he had to be able truthfully to say of himself; and an unshakable belief in divine justice, coupled with the intensity of his desire for everlasting life, was the incentive which ever impelled him, even unwillingly, towards benevolence.

Then again it was the Egyptian belief that the ghost or astral body, after the death of the moral man, required the attentions of the living to ensure its comfort. The dead were dependent, for a time at any rate, on the good-will of the living: prayers on their behalf were necessary, food and drink-offerings had to be supplied to them, and a kindly memory of them had to survive, so that their invisible presence in the earthly homes they had left might be loved and welcomed. Thus it was very necessary that their fellow-men should bear them no grudge nor ill-will; and hence all acts of cruelty were carefully avoided. Over and over again the Egyptians declared in their mortuary inscriptions that they had harmed no one, for by this means they hoped to encourage the charity of future generations.

Here, for example, is the statement of an old soldier

of princely rank, named Intef, who lived about 1450 B.C. "I was a man," he says, "who shortened the hour of the cruel, and obliged the wickedly minded to conform to the laws; who was gentle to the nervous, understanding their hearts, and knowing their thoughts before the words came forth from their lips. I was the servant of the poor, the father of the fatherless, the protector of the weak, and the husband of the widow, making the sorrowful happy."

And here are like declarations made by great princes who lived many centuries earlier. "There was no citizen's daughter whom I misused," states one of these, "there was no widow whom I afflicted; there was no peasant whom I evicted; there was none wretched amongst my people; there was none hungry in my time." "Never," says another, "did I do anything unkind to anybody." "Never," declares a third, "did I do violence to any man."

Prince Ptah-hotpe, 2600 B.C., wrote: "Do not try to frighten people, for it effects nothing, since what God has decreed happens." King Akhtoi, 2200 B.C., addressed his son as follows: "Put not your faith in length of years, for the gods of Judgment regard a lifetime as but an hour, and a man's deeds are laid beside him as his only treasure. Eternal is the existence yonder, and a fool is he who makes light of it. Do justice, therefore; comfort the mourner; oppress not the widow; take care that you do not punish wrongfully; and do not kill, for it will not profit you. Rule men as God's little flock, for they are His own images, proceeding from Him. When they weep He hears, and He knows every one of us by name. Kill nobody, for God, in whose care he is, commends him to you."

An engineer of about 1900 B.C. says: "I managed my workmen with great kindness: I did not shout at them." A prince of about the same date, who had to have a heavy colossus hauled for many miles, writes: "The road by which the statue had to come was very difficult, and the hauling of it would have been trying to the spirit of the people; so I caused a new road to be made, and very good it was to see how happily the men worked, and how everybody shouted and sang." King Thutmose III, about 1450 B.C., tells us that his very prisoners-of-war loved him, and that he "supplied them with bread, beer, and every sort of good food."

This same King is known to have pardoned his enemies on many occasions; and the leniency of other monarchs stands on record, as, for example, when Kink Intefoe, 1650 B.C., only banished, but did not execute, a traitor who had raised a rebellion against him. After a big sea-fight, about 1100 B.C., we have it on record that the Egyptian sailors rescued the crews of the enemy's sinking ships; and we read of a later King begging his enemies in a besieged city to submit "so that the children weep not," and especially so that the horses shall not starve.

The Egyptians, indeed, were tender-hearted to an astonishing extent; and that being so, let me urge the film-producer, should he feel impelled to wallow for a while in the sink of ancient iniquity, to leave out of the picture these humane dwellers on the banks of the Nile. The bestial, half-naked, hairy-chested executioner, beloved of Hollywood, did not exist in Egypt; the gigantic black slave with the red-hot tongs in his hand, or the terrible whip upraised, was unknown there; and the fiendish Pharaoh casting screaming girls to the crocodiles exists only in the heated imagination of the producer. I am spoiling his diabolical fun, I know; but there it is. . . .

VII

THE RESULT OF SMACKING QUEEN BOADICEA

I ONCE happened to state in a newspaper article that the celebrated British Queen Boadicea, who nearly succeeded in driving the Roman legions out of Britain in A.D. 61, revolted in the first place because a Roman officer had smacked her; by which I meant to indicate that I did not believe the more orthodox story that she had been officially "beaten with rods." But during the following days I received about a score of letters from readers of that particular newspaper, protesting that I was making fun of one of England's national heroines, and that it was undignified in an historian to write thus lightly about a queen being smacked.

It was evident, in fact, that nothing short of a formal flogging of this royal lady could be regarded as compatible with the dignity of history; and I was feeling more than usually ungentlemanly when I received a letter from a personage, apparently a medium, saying that he had just had a chat with Boadicea, who was as pleasant-spoken a lady as you could wish to meet, and that she had fully confirmed what I had said, frankly admitting that she had been slapped, not beaten.

I may add that those who have read my *Life and Times of Cleopatra,* and have deemed her dignity to be impinged by my treatment, will be interested to hear that I received recently a scented missive from New York, unsigned, but reading: "Cleopatra, reincarnated upon earth, has read your book, and thanks you"; while no less than eleven other ladies have secretly confessed to me that they are Cleopatra, and are not offended.

Feeling, then, that my knowledge of women is reliable, I am emboldened to tell here the story of Queen Boadicea, or Boudicca as she should more properly be called, and to repeat that she was not actually beaten; but it must be admitted at the outset that the description of her, as given by Dion Cassius, is not exactly that of a woman one would slap. She was, he says, "tall in figure and frightening in appearance; her voice was harsh and her expression savage; around her neck was a heavy band of twisted gold; over her bosom a striped vest was tightly pulled, while above this she wore a thick cloak fastened with a brooch or clasp; and her hair, which was yellow, hung down over all to her waist-belt."

Her people were the Iceni (probably pronounced *Ikny,* with the hard Latin C), a race of Belgic origin which had crossed over to Britain some two hundred years earlier, and had made a little kingdom of the

territory now known as Norfolk and Suffolk, with its
capital at Caistor St. Edmund, between two and three
miles south of Norwich (called by the Romans *Venta
Icenorum*). The Iceni seem to have been great horse-
breeders, and there is reason to suppose that they did
much business with the other British kingdoms, being
well spoken of, influential, powerful and prosperous.

Now, when the Romans invaded Britain in A.D. 43
they marched at once on Colchester, the old Camu-
lodunum, that being the royal city of Caratacu., King
of the Trinovantes, the most important leader on the
British side, son of the famous Cunobeline or Cymbe-
line; and the Emperor Claudius was himself present
when the legions, accompanied by a great number of
elephants (the tanks of those days), made their
triumphal entry into this city, where he received the
submission of the neighbouring kings, no doubt including that of Prasutagus, King of the Iceni, Boudicca's
husband.

A Roman *colonia,* or colony of ex-soldiers, was soon
established at Colchester; and thus the kingdom of the
Iceni, whose frontier was but a few miles away, came
very much under Roman eyes, and presently was overrun by Roman officials, soldiers and settlers. Reports of
the lucrative horse-dealing business carried on by these
people seem at length to have reached Rome, where the
great financiers were always on the look-out for a
profitable investment of their money. Anything to do

with the newly acquired province of Britain was at
that time very popular in the imperial city, and it may
be that some of the horses of the Iceni were taken over
to Italy, for it was certainly the fashion there to drive
about in British chariots. Roman ladies, too, began to
dye their hair yellow so as to look like British women;
and it is quite possible that reports of Queen Boudicca's
golden tresses had something to do with the craze.

There lived at this time in Rome the famous Stoic
philosopher, Seneca, the man who wrote all those charming essays on the subject of the simple life and the
cultivation of a mind raised high above thoughts of
worldly wealth and position. He was at this time engaged in the accumulation of a fortune, and being not
averse from a little quiet money-lending, he managed
to induce King Prasutagus and Queen Boudicca to
accept a cash-advance from him. Prasutagus, however,
died a few years later without a son to succeed him, and
it was found in his will that he had taken the not
unusual step of making the Emperor his heir with his
two daughters, a formality which, for reasons which I
need not explain, was expected to have the effect of
ensuring the continuity of his royal line as a vassal
dynasty under imperial protection.

There appears to have been, however, some legal
point in this settlement which endangered Seneca's
money, and he therefore called in the loan, just at a
time when the widowed Boudicca was not too com-

fortably off. Tacitus says, too, that "all the principal
lords of the Iceni had been deprived of their hereditary
estates" by the Romans, mainly, I suppose, because they,
likewise, had borrowed money and in one way and
another had got into the clutches of Roman financiers.
The little nation, in fact, had been pretty ruthlessly
exploited, and I expect that Prasutagus had given Roman
company-promoters all kinds of concessions which had
resulted in the fleecing of his people.

Then, one day, Boudicca discovered that her daugh-
ters were having "affairs" with Roman officers; and the
Queen, naturally enough, put the blame on the men.
There was a great to-do about it, no doubt; and it was
perhaps during one of the scenes which followed that
Boudicca was smacked by a Roman.

Tacitus states that she was given a formal beating,
but this is extremely unlikely. She was under the protection of the Emperor, and it would have been all
against the policy of Rome in Britain thus to maltreat
a vassal queen, so soon after the country had been received into the Empire with great enthusiasm as a
wealthy and highly civilized group of states—some of
whose princes, too, were popular figures in Roman
society, and whose fighting qualities, moreover, were
well known to the Roman Governor, Suetonius Paulinus. It is far more probable that Boudicca, while
pouring out her wrongs to some unresponsive official,
or while arguing with one of Seneca's or the Emperor's

personal agents, threw a vase of something at the man's head, or boxed his ears, with the result that there was a disorderly scene during which she also received a slap or blow of some kind, whereat I suppose she went storming from the room, shouting out that she had been struck.

The consequences were appalling. The whole nation of the Iceni flew to arms, and, like a swarm of bees, fell upon the Roman colony at Colchester. The Romans living there had made a very comfortable little settlement for themselves: they had built a temple dedicated to the Emperor Claudius, they had erected a town-hall and a theatre, and their pretty houses were grouped all around. But rumours of the rising of the Iceni had reached them a few days before the attack, and their nerves were so strung up that the wildest stories of portents predicting disaster were circulated. Somebody said that ghostly whisperings had been heard in the town-hall; others assembled at the theatre were scared by sounds of dreadful howling which could not be accounted for; and so forth.

When the horde of Iceni horsemen appeared at the city's gates, and were received as allies by the Trinovantes, the Romans hastily fortified the temple, the women and children taking refuge in the great vaults beneath it which you may still visit under the Norman castle; and there, after a two days' siege, they were all most brutally massacred and the city was burnt. The

Iceni then marched on Verulamium (St. Albans), burning that place also, and slaughtering the Roman settlers.
Thereupon the Ninth Legion, recruited in Spain and
now stationed at Lincoln, marched southwards, only
to be nearly wiped out by Boudicca's men, who, after
their victory, marched on London, their Queen riding
at their head in her war-chariot.

Suetonius Paulinus, the Governor, was away in North
Wales at the time of the rising, but he marched his two
Legions, the Fourteenth and Twentieth, at top speed
to London, arriving there just ahead of the enemy.
The citizens implored him to defend the city, but this,
for some strategic reason now forgotten, he was unable
to do, and London was burnt to the ground, after which
Boudicca led her army against the relieving force which
had taken up a strong position outside the city—some
think near the modern King's Cross.

Certain of victory, she drew up her baggage wagons
in the rear of her troops, quite close to the Romans, and
having harangued her men and worked them into a
frenzy, gave orders for a frontal attack; but this time
she found herself opposed to 10,000 of Rome's finest
soldiers, and although the Iceni outnumbered them by
at least ten to one, they were utterly annihilated, and
even the women and camp-followers in the wagons,
and all the horses, were slaughtered.

Therefore Boudicca, refusing to surrender or to survive her subjects, swallowed poison and thus ended her

violent life. Seneca, I take it, never got his money back.

In British history the queen rightly stands out as a great figure, but I picture her as an uncontrolled woman of fierce temper, inspired by the wildest hatred of the Romans; and, as the instigator or abetter of the most awful massacres, during which Roman ladies were stripped naked and tortured before being murdered, she can hardly be termed a pleasant character. It may be that I am prejudiced against her by the description Dion Cassius gives of her appearance; but really she arouses in me no patriotic enthusiasm. Big, golden-haired women in tight jumpers always appal me.

VIII

THE STRANGE CASE OF AARON THE ORTHODOX

In Arabic the name Aaron is *Harûn*, and the word "orthodox" is *rashîd*; and the reader who has never heard of anybody called Aaron the Orthodox, and, indeed, finds in the name little promise of entertainment, will be relieved to discover in him our old friend of The Arabian Nights, Haroun Alraschid, or, more properly, Harûn er-Rashîd, Caliph of Baghdad from A.D. 786 to 809. But I have used the less attractive name for a purpose: I want to dissociate the tragic figure which history reveals to us, and which is here to be portrayed, from the romantic hero of the fairy-tales.

There is little romance about the real man. He was at first just what his name implies—an extremely devout and orthodox Moslem, always reading in the Korân the stories about Abraham, Moses, Aaron, and the other sacred old figures of long ago, and always immensely proud of the fact that he was sixth in descent from the Prophet's uncle; but, towards the end of his short life, he was a nervous wreck, his hands stained with blood, and his heart wrung with anguish. The story of his fall

from grace is very strange, very terrible; but the explanation of the tragedy is so hard to determine that
the reader will, I trust, find in the puzzle sufficient reason
for this excursion of ours to the Baghdad of over eleven
hundred years ago.

At the time of this Caliph's accession to the throne,
the city was not more than four-and-twenty years old
in its resuscitated form as a great Persian metropolis;
but already its population numbered well over a million,
and it had no rival in the vast Persian Empire. The
neighbourhood being devoid of timber or good building-
stone, the houses were constructed of brick and were
richly ornamented with decorative tiles; and the size
and fine grouping of these brightly coloured buildings,
the splendid streets and open squares, and the many
artificial gardens and fountains, made it the wonder of
the Orient.

Its wealth was fabulous, and its trade enormous, one
of its chief products being the silk manufactured in the
Attabieh quarter, from which name, by the way, is
derived our word "tabby," now only applied to the
humbler species of cat, but once having the meaning of
the brindled or streaked pattern in rich native fabric.
Life was lived sumptuously in this magnificent city, and
the pomp of the Caliph's court had no equal in the
world.

There were three great empires in existence in those
days. There was the Roman empire of the west, over

which Charlemagne ruled with the sanction of the Pope, his dominions including Rome itself and most of western Europe; there was the Greek empire centred in Constantinople, which incorporated Venice and part of Southern Italy, and which was governed by the Christian Emperor Nicephorus; and there was this huge Persian empire, the greatest of the three, under the dominion of the Caliph, who was not only King and Emperor but Commander of the Faithful and God's Vicar on earth, whose slightest word was law throughout the lands of Persia as far as the frontiers of India and Tartary, throughout Syria, Palestine, and Arabia, and throughout Egypt and all North Africa to the shores of Spain and the far-off Atlantic.

The Caliph is known to have sent an embassy bearing rich presents to the Court of Charlemagne; but Nicephorus he treated with disdain, invading his territory no less than eight times. Once the Greek Emperor wrote to him saying that he would no longer pay the tribute of 30,000 gold pieces which had been exacted annually as the price of peace with Islâm; but to this the Caliph replied: "In the name of God, the Merciful, the Compassionate, Harûn er-Rashîd, Commander of the Faithful, to Nicephorus, the Greek dog: I have read your letter, you son of an unbelieving mother, and you shall not hear, you shall *see,* my reply," dispatching after this terse message an army which was completely victorious.

Born in the year 766, the Caliph was but twenty-one

years of age when he came to the throne; and he at once placed all the affairs of the empire in the hands of a certain Yahya, a man of Persian blood. Under the rule of this enlightened Prime Minister the Persians, though regarded as of inferior race, came into much prominence, the Caliph, however, and most of his nobles being Arabs, and Arabic being the court language. This Yahya had two sons, Al Fadhl, and Jafar, the Jaafer of the Arabian Nights; and the latter became the bosom friend of the Caliph. The monarch loved this young man with a passionate and jealous devotion which may be the key to the mystery of the events about to be related; and there are many tales illustrating their intimacy, amongst which, however, I need only cite that wherein it is related how a cloak was caused to be made having two neck-holes, so that the two friends might wrap themselves in a single garment.

The Caliph was married to his own cousin, Zobiedeh, who, however, played no great part in his life. As an instance of the piety of the palace, I may mention that a hundred girls were employed in the *harîm*, or women's quarters, whose business it was to intone the scriptures all day long, so that the place is described as having been like a beehive, always full of humming and droning. But great magnificence went with this piety, and Zobiedeh was accompanied wherever she went by a bodyguard of girls, dressed as pages, a fashion which was afterwards copied by all the smart ladies of Baghdad. Her private meals were served on gold plate; but her husband's banquets relied more on the brilliancy of the company for their success, and often he would sit talking till sunrise, while Abu Nawas, his jester, slept at his feet.

Now the Caliph had a sister, Abbasah, whom he loved as much as he did Jafar; and around these two his whole emotional life revolved. They were the apples of his eyes, and he desired above all things to be able to have them both about him in the private apartments of the palace without any of those restraints which convention imposed where a woman was concerned. It seemed to him intolerable that Abbasah should always have modestly to retire when Jafar entered; and therefore he conceived the plan of marrying them to one another, so that his friend should be able to have access, like himself, at all times to the *harîm*, and should be in every way one of the family.

On the other hand, it was not fitting that Jafar, who was a mere Persian, should mate with a lady of the imperial Arabic house, with its pure and holy descent from the family of the Prophet: and therefore the Caliph exacted an oath from these two that their marriage should be merely formal, and that they would not have any actual relationship closer than that of the triple friendship he had set his heart upon.

So it was arranged; but the Caliph, being a most pious Moslem, used to go almost every year on pilgrimage to Mecca. Nine times he accomplished the long journey, which he always made on foot, prostrating himself on the ground one hundred times each morning and evening when he said his prayers; but while he was thus away from home, for months at a time, Abbasah, being only human, made an actual husband of Jafar, and bore him two sons, of whose existence—according to the rather improbable story current in Baghdad— the Caliph knew nothing.

Meanwhile the court became ever more famous as the home of wit and beauty, and the centre of intellectuality and art. The sovereign himself was a scholar of high standing, who introduced to the Arabic world the learning of the ancient Greeks, and who took especial delight in poetry. The greatest figures in literature, the leading scientists, the most noted philosophers, and the most famous divines, gathered about his table; and there are many stories telling how he honoured them, in one instance actually waiting upon a certain blind poet, and washing the man's hands for him.

But all the time the high-standing and wealth of Jafar increased, until his influence became even more important than that of his father, Yahya, and indeed, his authority was at length almost equal to the Caliph's. His palace was the most luxurious in the whole land, for the sovereign's own tastes were more simple; and there is a story that the very floors were studded with pearls and rubies, and the ceilings with amber, while a

single robe of honour worn by him was so thickly sewn
with jewels that its value was nearly £200,000. There
are hundreds of tales which reveal his munificence and
his power; but I have space here to mention only one
of them.

A certain rogue who had gone on a visit to Egypt,
forged for himself a letter of introduction to the
Governor of that country, supposed to have been written by Jafar, with whom this Governor had lately been
on bad terms; and the latter, regarding it as a sort of
olive branch, lavishly entertained the perpetrator of the
forgery, being very willing thus to end the quarrel. But
after a while something aroused his suspicions, and he
sent the letter to Baghdad to be verified, the deception
thus being discovered by Jafar. He, however, was delighted to find that his enemy had thus shown his desire
to end their feud, and therefore wrote to him, saying:
"Good God!—how could you think that my letter was
a forgery?—it is in my own handwriting, and the bearer
is one of my most intimate friends." The Governor
showed this letter to the perplexed miscreant, apologiz-
ing thereafter to the astounded man for having doubted
his credentials; and ultimately he sent him back in
state, loaded with gifts, to Baghdad, where Jafra completed his utter bewilderment by making him enormous
presents as having served, if unwittingly, the pacificatory schemes of God.

Then suddenly, came the terrible events which

wrecked the happiness of the Caliph. People said that he had just found out that Jafar and Abbasah had really been living as man and wife, and, moreover, that the vast wealth and dangerous power of his friend had only now become known to him. Added to this, they said. he had lately learnt that the young man was at heart an atheist.

But all these explanations seem to be very improbable. We only know for certain that he called his executioner, the famous Mesrûr of the Arabian Nights, and gasped out an order to him to go and kill the Princess Abbasah; and, when the deed was done, he sat there weeping bitterly in her room, while his men buried her beneath the floor. Next he sent for Jafar, and ordered Mesrûr to behead him; and when the head was brought to him, he wept over it, and muttered bitter reproaches to it, digging his walking-stick savagely into the ground after each sentence, and grinding his teeth.

After that, he caused the two sons of this secret union to be brought to him; and having sobbed over them, had them both killed and buried beside their mother under the floor, at the same time calling down God's vengeance on his own head for having murdered them. Then he arrested Yahya, and Jafar's brother, Al Fadhl, and had them imprisoned, forbidding anybody to mention their names again. Both men died in captivity, the one of infirmity and old age, and the other of cancer of the tongue; but when Yahya was on his deathbed he

wrote a note to the Caliph, saying just this: "The ac-
cuser is going on ahead to the Tribunal; the accused will
follow shortly"—on reading which the monarch fainted.

Later, when the Caliph was asked why he had acted
thus, he replied: "If this shirt which I am wearing knew
the real reason, I would tear it to pieces," meaning to
say that he would never reveal the secret.

From that time onwards he wasted away, a neu-
rasthenic ruin of a man, shocking to see. Daily he wept
floods of tears; often he fainted; and he declared that
the hand of every man was turned against him, even
his two sons being suspected. His administration of his
realms became chaotic, and there were many rebellions.
In the case of the last revolt against him, the captured
rebel leader having been brought before him, the once
notoriously merciful Caliph muttered: "If I had no
more time left me to live than would suffice to move
my lips, I would say 'kill him!'" and he ordered his
soldiers to hack the man to pieces, but fell unconscious
from his throne at the first stroke of their swords. He
died a few days later, at the age of forty-three; and
his secret was buried with him.

IX

THE GREAT PYRAMID

A SHORT time ago I received through the post a pamphlet advertising somebody's book about the Great Pyramid, wherein is set forth its "divine message," and we are told that the real architect was the Almighty Himself, the actual builder probably being Shem, and that the measurements and arrangements of the passages and chambers reveal the essential features of our Christian religion, the most important scientific facts necessary to our understanding of the universe, and the chief dates in the world's history from the time of Adam down to the establishment of the Irish Free State.

I cannot give here the name of the book, for the pamphlet has now passed beyond recall from my waste-paper basket to that dim region of oblivion served by the dust-carts; and, indeed, the reference would not be of much moment, since everybody is aware, I suppose, that this huge tomb of the Pharaoh Cheops is widely believed to contain all manner of startling secrets hid from scholars and revealed to evangelical visionaries. But, it has occurred to me that the Great Pyramid, if only because of its complete innocence of most of the symbolism so often attributed to it in these wonder-loving days, provides a good subject for discussion in these pages.

This, however, is no place for argument, and I shall not attempt to break a lance with the writer of the pamphlet, and of the book it advertises. I propose only to take the reader with me on our magic carpet away across the seas and back through the centuries, until we reach the city of Memphis and find ourselves being conveyed along its sunny streets one breezy October morning in the year 2770 B.C., that is to say about three years before the building of the Great Pyramid was completed.

We will suppose ourselves to have become the guests of one of the important overseers of the work, a corpulent old gentleman, wearing no more to hide his brown nakedness than a white linen skirt or kilt around his middle. He has close-cropped grey hair, his face is clean-shaven, and in his hand he carries a long staff: you may see his exact counterpart in the famous statue known as the Shêkh-el-Beled now in the Cairo Museum, though the personage there represented lived a couple of generations or so later than the time of Cheops.

Cheops!—it is an ugly name, and our host would not be likely to recognize it, for the –s is a later termination added by the Greeks, and the p was originally f, the Pharaoh being really called Cheof or Kheuf, which is not so ill-sounding, and has the comfortable meaning

"He protects," the reference being to the old ram-headed potter who was the patron deity and protector of the little town where the Pharaoh was born.

Memphis, too, is a name which has suffered a change; for the –*is,* is a Greek addition, and the remaining Memph is a corruption of the original Mennofr, "the Established in Beauty," as the city was called in the remote ages to which we have penetrated.

Our portly friend, beaming with the historic kindliness of the Egyptian people, is seated in a carrying chair railed around like a child's cot, and set upon long shafts supported on the shoulders of four men; and we, too, having been provided with similar conveyances, smile affably about us from a like height above the glare of the hot roadways, our only regret being that we have left our blue spectacles in 1928.

We are proceeding, of course, up into the desert to have a look at Ikhut, "the Glorious Seat," which is the name of the pyramid; and the morning sun is behind us as we move westward out of the town and across the fields towards the low hills of sand and white limestone rocks which form the horizon.

Presently as we mount up into the dazzling desert we can turn and look back upon the capital—a great cluster of whitewashed houses set amidst the flat expanse of the fields and groves of palm-trees, some distance back from the Nile. The city, so our guide explains, though one of the youngest in Egypt, is already

over six centuries old; but signs of its age are hidden
by the liberal use of whitewash upon the walls of its
buildings, while, away to the left or south, the great
temple of Ptah, the Egyptian Vulcan, is bright with
paint of many colours, and looks in the distance like a
gaudy Russian toy.

The dusty roadway brings us out at length up on to
the high ground of the desert, and now a solitary white
pyramid, built in a series of great steps, comes into
view, standing stark against the azure sky, and rising
from the golden sand which stretches away to north,
south, and west, as far as the eye can see. This is the
last resting-place of the Pharaoh Thoser, who died nearly
a hundred years before our visit; but when we exclaim
at its huge proportions our guide smiles in a superior
manner, and points his hand towards the north, where,
nine miles away, the unfinished top of another solitary
pyramid rises above the folds of the hills. That is Ikhut,
he tells us; and we settle ourselves in our chairs for the
two hours' journey to it, happy now to have the cool
north wind blowing in our faces from the far-off
Mediterranean.

One of our first questions is as to why the Pharaoh
had chosen this particular spot, ten miles from his
capital as the site of his tomb, and the answer we receive
is threefold. Firstly, there is here an extensive and flat
plateau of rock which was seen to be eminently suitable
for the building of this vast structure. Secondly, it is

situated just at the meeting-place of the two original
Egyptian Kingdoms, the long, narrow valley of Upper
Egypt here suddenly spreading out into the wide Delta
of Lower Egypt; and thus the Pharaoh could feel that
from this point of vantage his spirit would for ever be
able to watch over the two united realms. And thirdly,
the site is equidistant between Memphis and On, the
sacred city of the Sun; and, in the great rivalry between
the two places, no one could say that the Pharaoh had
favoured one or other, but rather that he had departed
an equal distance from both to find a position for his
lonely and tremendous tomb.

And why, we ask, did he choose to build his sepulchre
in the form of a pyramid? To this our host has a twofold
answer. In the first place the pyramid may be regarded
as a natural development from the shape of earlier
tombs. At the outset, in the far-off days, there was the
tomb in the form of a pit with a mound of sand above
it; then, when stone structures began to be made, a
deeper sepulchral pit was cut into the underlying rock,
and over it a rectangular, flat-topped mound of masonry
was built; next, this masonry construction was increased
in area and used as the base for a similar but smaller
structure set on top of it, which became in its turn
the base of yet another and still smaller structure erected
above it again, and so on, until we have Thoser's pyramid, which looks like a flight of monstrous steps rising

on four sides to a central pinnacle. The advance from this to the new idea of a perfect pyramid was natural, and only required the filling in of the steps.

In the second place, there is that most holy stone of the Sun in the sacred court of the temple of On; and this monolith which is in the form of a pyramidion, or small pyramid, and which is called the Benben, is itself a development of the original cairn or mound of stones once used as the altar of the sun-worshippers. Thus the Pharaoh, in constructing his tomb in the novel form of a huge Benben, and arranging to have himself encased inside it, could feel that he would for ever be shut into, and would become a part of, a vast symbol of the Sun-god, who was his divine ancestor and the protector of the royal line.

When did the work on this great pyramid begin, we ask? Our host replies that it began very shortly after the Pharaoh's accession (that is to say in the year 2789 B.C.) nearly twenty years ago; but he tells us that actual building operations have only lasted for three months in each year, namely, during the seasons of the Nile-floods, from the middle of August to the middle of November, when labour could be commandeered from all parts of the country without interfering with agriculture. During the other nine months in each year, some ten thousand quarrymen have been busy extracting the blocks of stone from the hills on the opposite side of the Nile, and stacking them on to the water's edge, ready for transport by raft on the floods which in the autumn extend right across the river-valley and lap the foot of the plateau whereon the pyramid is being built.

And how, we want to know, are the stones raised? "Look for yourselves," he replies; for now we are close enough to this mighty mountain of masonry to see that its outer surface is enveloped with a maze of sloping pathways, zigzagging up it on all sides, solidly built of sun-dried mud bricks, which will be removed when the job is finished. Along these paths thousands of men are swarming in little groups of twenties and thirties, each group dragging up into its required position a single block of stone resting upon a sort of sledge.

Each side of the pyramid has a 755-foot frontage at the base; and the overseer tells us that about 10,000 men are assigned thereto, which means to say that, taking the average over the twenty years, if each group of thirty men has dragged one stone to its place in one day, more than 300 blocks have been able to be laid each day on each face, or 1200 blocks on all four faces. Now, this rate of work, he explains, has not proved arduous to those working on the building, nor to the quarrymen, since the latter have only been called upon to provide enough blocks for about one hundred days of building-work in each year, that is to say 120,000 blocks, and that number, spread over twelve months, has meant that not more than 300 or 350 blocks have had to be quarried each day. Ten men can get out one block in three days or less, and thus about 10,000 men have been able easily to produce the required daily number.

But, says the old fellow, spreading out his hands, the organization of the work, involving the employment of some 70,000 men, has been simply marvellous; and now the last part of the business, namely, the careful building of the smooth outer casing of the whole structure, is going to require a degree of skill infinitely greater than that necessary in the earlier phases. However, he declares, by favour of the gods the pyramid will be finished in another two years; and we do not use our knowledge of the future to warn him that that will be none too soon, the Pharaoh being destined to reign no more than twenty-three years (the evidence for which will be found on pages 13 and 165 of the first volume of my *History of the Pharaohs*).

By this time we have reached the works, and are being carried around this huge mountain as yet lacking its apex. The smell of beer and onions is brought to our nostrils on the spanking north wind, and we learn that the men have not long finished their mid-morning meal. They are a noisy, happy multitude, and the air is filled with shouting and laughter, and the echoing lilt of their many hauling-songs. The foremen scold and gesticulate, wildly waving their whips, it is true, but they do not seem to use them on the labourers' backs, and there is that same good humour which characterize gang-work on the banks of the Nile in the twentieth century Anno Domini.

But what about the divine significance of the measurements of the pyramid, we ask our host, and its mystic orientation in relation to the stars, and its symbolic exposition of the fall of Adam, and the consequent handicap of the human race?

"Fudge!" is his reply. Egyptians are a practical people, he laughs; and by carrying out this great idea of erecting an eternal mortuary monument which shall stagger humanity, the Pharaoh has only acted in accordance with his perfectly legitimate views as to his and Egypt's pre-eminence in the world, and incidentally he has kept a great army of his subjects occupied, well fed, and hard as nails, during the lazy months of the annual season of inundation. There have been no complaints.

"And anyway," our host adds, "who is Adam? I have never heard of him."

X

THE TRAGEDY OF CLEOMENES

THE more closely one studies ancient history the more closely one realizes that what is called civilization has no connection with humaneness. A nation can be highly organized, can produce great works of art, erect magnificent buildings, live under luxurious conditions, and yet be no better than a pack of cut-throats. Even a high state of intellectual civilization, as revealed by wide learning and a large literary output, does not necessarily imply any proper understanding of man's prime obligation, his duty towards his neighbour.

The real token of a nation's enlightenment is its recognition of the rights of every living creature, its benevolence, its pity, and its abhorrence of causing unnecessary suffering; but mere "civilization" does not pay much regard to such matters. The Assyrians were highly civilized, yet they flayed their enemies alive on the battlefield, and impaled them on sharp stakes, leaving them there to squirm until death provided the mercy denied by the living. The Cæsars were highly civilized, yet they perpetrated the most abominable cruelties on man and beast.

Let us take a look at the highly civilized Greeks of
the third century B.C., addressing ourselves particularly
to the adventures of the royal house of cultured Sparta;
and we shall be witnesses of a series of horrors which
could hardly be equalled in the most benighted corners
of the earth. We shall see that these precious Greeks
have no idea of the rudiments of human obligation;
and thus we shall learn one of the most important lessons which Antiquity has to teach, namely, that mankind cannot be said to have placed its feet upon the path
of progress until something far greater than "civilization" directs its course.

In the year 240 B.C. the gentle and upright young
Agis the Fourth, twenty-ninth King of Sparta of the
Agid line, was kidnapped by agents of the government,
an oligarchy often at loggerheads with the sovereign,
and was hustled off to prison, where he was submitted
to a mock trial. His mother and grandmother, meanwhile, having located him, stood outside the prison gates,
screaming and waving their arms about, while a sympathetic crowd gathered around them; but their action
only served to hasten the death of the King, for his
captors, fearing that he might be rescued, determined
on his immediate execution, and he was secretly
strangled.

One of the government officials then went out to the
crowd, declaring that the King was unharmed, and
thereupon the two royal ladies implored him to allow

them to go into the prison to see the unfortunate youth, a request which was at once granted. The King's grandmother, an aged woman of the highest character, was first conducted to the chamber where the murder had taken place, but no sooner had she entered than a noose was slipped around her poor old neck, and she was swung off her feet and hanged.

Next they brought in his mother, and callously showed her the old lady swaying there at the end of a rope, and the body of her son lying on the ground. Then they told her that they were going to hang her also, to which she calmly replied that she hoped it would redound to the good of Sparta; and after she had helped to lay out the two bodies decently, she submitted herself quietly to the executioner, and was quickly dispatched.

Leonidas the Second, another member of the royal house, who had been a party to the crime, and now found himself sole ruler of Sparta, had a son, Cleomenes, still a boy; and to this lad he married the distraught and protesting widow of the murdered King Agis, because she happened to be very wealthy. She, however, is said to have become quite fond of her new husband in the end; for Cleomenes was not unkind to her, and always spoke of Agis with respect. He had been educated by a Stoic philosopher, and had cultivated a stern silent manner, using the Laconic, or Spartan, method of address, and being frugal in his habits.

In 236 B.C. this Cleomenes succeeded to the throne, and at first showed great friendliness to the group of men who had supported his father, going so far as to oblige his widowed mother, Cratesiclea, to marry one of them. Later, however, he turned upon them, and had them all massacred in cold blood one day as they sat at table together.

After that he began to try to reintroduce into Sparta that ancient and ridiculous discipline which had fallen out of fashion. The early Spartans had made a fetish of communistic discipline. When a child was born it was taken to the local council, who decided whether it should be reared or murdered. If it was a boy and was considered fit to live, the parents were allowed to keep their son until he was seven years of age, after which he belonged to the State, and was educated by government instructors until he was twenty, being thrashed at intervals, and made to endure every kind of hardship, at the same time being put through a long course of physical jerks and gymnastics, to which were added dancing, music, and the usual lessons of the school of the period. From twenty to thirty he had to serve in the army, and later he had to do with the work assigned to him, until at sixty he was pensioned off.

Every male was obliged to marry, but the State chose the bride, and always restricted the man's relations with her, the girls having been taught from earliest childhood to regard husbands and sons as belonging, body and soul, to the State. All meals were communal; no money was allowed to be handled; no private business could be engaged in; and all forms of Capitalism were penalized.

These communistic rules and regulations, which never did the least good to Sparta, had been in abeyance for many years at the time when Cleomenes attempted to put them into force again; and his success was limited. He tried, too, to make his country the leading state in the Peloponnese, if not in all Greece; and soon he was at war with the Achæan League, a confederacy of other states, led by a certain Aratus. This Aratus, by the way, had as a youth escaped the general murder of his family, but in the end was himself murdered.

The war went badly for Cleomenes, who was at last obliged to seek the aid of the Greek army of Ptolemy the Third, the Grecian King of Egypt. Ptolemy, however, only consented to help him on condition that his children and Cratesiclea, his mother, should be sent as hostages to Alexandria, the Greek capital of Egypt, so that if Cleomenes should play him false there would be some important people to murder in revenge.

The Spartan sovereign could not at first make up his mind to broach the matter to Cratesiclea, but she soon perceived that there was something troubling him, and when at last he told her of King Ptolemy's terms she put her arms about him, and, with a laugh, said: "Was this the thing that you were afraid to tell me?— make haste, and put me on board ship, and send this body where it may be of service to Sparta, before age destroys it unprofitably here at home."

So it was arranged, and mother and son with many tears bade farewell in the temple of Neptune at Tae-narus; but, as they left the building, the brave old lady wiped her eyes, and drawing herself up, said: "King of Sparta, when we come out at the door, let no one see us weeping or showing any emotion unworthy of Sparta!"

Cratesiclea and her grandchildren resided at Alex-andria for many years; but Cleomenes was finally de-feated by his enemies at the battle of Sellasia in 222 B.C., and fled for his life to the Egyptian capital, where he was honourably entertained by his ally. A few months later, however, this monarch died, and was succeeded by Ptolemy the Fourth, the most dissolute of the Greek Kings of Egypt, who soon had many murders to his account, including those of his mother, brother, and wife, the last-named being done to death by special request of his mistress, Agathocleia.

This unpleasant young man was extremely cultured, and wrote quite a fine tragedy in the style of Euripides; and, having an ingenious imagination, he organized all manner of revelries and orgies, amongst which I may mention a most diverting round-up of the Jews, who, had the plan not miscarried, were to be trampled to death in the circus by intoxicated elephants.

At length King Ptolemy turned his attention to Cleomenes, whose presence in his capital he regarded as a menace to peace, and whose Spartan habits he could not abide; and soon he had him safe in custody, together with twelve of his exiled nobles. One day, however, they made a dash for it into the streets, shouting to the Alexandrian Greeks to help them to regain their liberty.

Nobody, however, would risk their skins to do so, and the escaped prisoners, after killing a few people to no purpose, decided to commit suicide, and one by one they drove their swords into their hearts. Panteus, a very handsome young noble, was the last to die; and, before he stabbed himself, he went from body to body as they lay, pricking each with his dagger to ascertain that life was extinct. But when he thus touched Cleomenes, the King groaned and turned over upon his back; whereupon Panteus sat down beside him, and kissed him, holding him in his arms, nor did he seek his own death until that of his sovereign was come.

King Ptolemy, hearing the news, ordered the body of Cleomenes to be skinned and hung above a gate of the city, and the women and children of his household to be slain. Now the beautiful young wife of Panteus was with Queen Cratesiclea, and when they were arrested it was she who comforted the old lady, and, as they were led to execution, held her aged hand.

Cratesiclea asked only that she might be killed before the children; but, with relentless cruelty, the Greek officers made her watch these beloved grandchildren of hers having their throats cut. "O children, whither are you gone?" she wailed as she saw them expire, and with those words upon her lips she, too, was murdered.

The wife of Panteus asked for a moment's respite, and, fastening her dress close about her for decency's sake, in silence and perfect composure closed the eyes of the dead and arranged them in a row. Then, turning to the executioner, she submitted herself quietly to his knife. . . .

I tell the story, ghastly though it be, for the purpose of illustrating the point I made at the beginning of this chapter. Civilization does not imply humaneness; and, as we have recently seen in the case of Russia, intellectuality and culture may go hand in hand with that very brutality which is the eternal enemy of mankind's salvation.

XI

THE REAL MOSES

THE Ancient Egyptian historian Manetho, whose
work has only survived in extracts used by other early
writers, states, in a quotation made by Eusebius, that
the Exodus of the Children of Israel from Egypt took
place immediately before the reign of the Pharaoh
Acherres, who seems to be identical with Ay, the successor of Tutankhamen. According to the system of
chronology which I have put forward in my *History of
the Pharaohs,* this would mean that Moses led the Israelites out of Egypt in about the year 1346 B.C.; and there
is a good deal to show that this is, in fact, the correct
date for that event. Moreover, the old Jewish historian
Josephus, in his book *Contra Apion,* again quoting from
Manetho, records a series of events recognizably those
which occurred in the reign of Akhnaton, Tutankhamen's predecessor; and he states that Moses took part
in them.

Assuming, then, that Manetho was basing his statements on authentic traditions—and, as I say, there is
much to show that this is so—the early life of Moses
must have been spent in the reign of the fat and jovial

Amenhotpe (Amenophis) the Third, Akhnaton's father; and if we accept Josephus's not improbable story that the great Hebrew law-giver was brought up as an Egyptian at the Pharaoh's palace, our very considerable knowledge of the royal court at that time will enable us to form a pretty substantial picture of his life when he was a young man. Let us therefore make the journey to Thebes, the Egyptian capital, in the days when this Amenhotpe was reigning, so that we may become acquainted with Moses, and obtain some idea of his appearance and habits.

The representations of him in mediæval and modern paintings and stained glass have so familiarized us with a bearded, long-haired figure in voluminous robes reaching to the ground, that it may be somewhat difficult for us to recognize him as a clean-shaven man who had short hair combed carefully back from his forehead, and who wore a loose-sleeved shirt of white linen open at the neck, and a sort of kilt extending below his knees, while on his feet were shoes with pointed toes. It may be rather startling, too, to find that when he went for a walk he put on a cap and a pair of gloves, and carried a walking-stick in his hand.

Priests, I should mention, had their heads as well as their faces shaved, and Moses is stated to have served for a while as a priest at Heliopolis; but other traditions present him as an ordinary gentleman of the time, having a high command in the Egyptian army, and therefore we may picture him, as I have just stated, with modern-looking short hair. On important occasions, however, he wore a heavy wig which hung down to his shoulders in a mass of black curls and plaits, and was in effect not unlike the long wigs worn by our ancestors of the days of Queen Anne.

This wig of his was thick with strongly scented pomade, and his skin was polished with a perfumed composition like soap, in which castor oil was the main ingredient. At parties, the servants constantly poured scent upon the guests' heads, handing round bunches or garlands of fragrant flowers; and scented pastilles were burnt in the rooms. The ladies, in the manner of those of modern times, often made use in public of a mirror and lip-stick, and in private of face-cream, rouge, eye-paint, and perfume; but Moses, like other gentlemen of the period, did no more in this respect than touch up his eyebrows and eyelashes, and sprinkle himself with scent, sometimes sucking a perfumed lozenge to counteract the smell of garlic on his breath.

Egyptians did not flop about on couches and divans in the day-time, but sat up, like honest men, on chairs of more or less modern shape. Moses, therefore, is to be pictured in his house, seated in this manner; but the chairs were often richly cushioned, and loose cushions of the ordinary drawing-room kind were lying about for use when he wished for extra comfort, while footstools were always handy. At night he slept upon a bedstead having a wooden frame, and a springy body made of cord threaded in a crisscross design, over which was a soft and pillow-like feather mattress. There was a canopy over this bed, supported on ornamental pillars of wood, and thus the whole thing was much like an ordinary four-poster.

He kept his clothes in wooden chests, or trunks made of wickerwork having trays inside, which could be lifted out and which were divided up into compartments for shirts, collars, handkerchiefs, and so forth. His wigs were kept in wig-boxes; other small boxes contained his comb and toilet articles, his scents, skin-foods, and face-creams, or his razor and the hone on which it was sharpened; and there were special boxes for his shoes.

At his meals he sat on a chair, with a low table before him whereon the glazed dishes and cups were spread; and near by were stands for the jars containing red and white wine, from which the cups were replenished. Sometimes a tube was inserted into one of these jars, and, whenever he wished to drink, a servant raised the other end to his lips so that he could suck at it without troubling to move. A mug of good strong beer, either light or dark, made from barley, was as popular as the wine; and he had no objection to a glass of milk.

Roast goose, duck, beef, and venison, were the usual

meats; a good deal of fish, cooked or dried, was eaten; crisp little onions, cucumbers, and celery were the chief relishes; there were many varieties of bread, rolls and cakes; and several kinds of fruit such as melons, figs, pomegranates, and grapes, were eaten; while honey was always in demand. At meal times a small washing-stand was placed near the table, whereon were a jug of scented water and a basin; for after anybody had been eating goose, for example, with his fingers, it was very necessary to wash his hands.

The royal palace where Moses was brought up stood at the edge of the desert on the west side of the Nile, opposite Thebes, the modern Luxor. It was some distance back from the river, and behind it towered the barren and magnificent hills of rock, golden against the blue sky. Extensive gardens had been laid out around it, and on the eastern side a huge pleasure-lake had been constructed, whereon the members of the court went out rowing or sailing in bottle boats—a very pleasant and romantic amusement on hot summer nights, when the moon or the stars were reflected in the water, and the scent of flowers was carried from the lamp-lit gardens on the gentle breeze.

The palace itself was a large, whitewashed brick building, containing many rooms, the plastered walls, floors, and ceilings being ornamented with charming paintings. Outside there were wide verandahs and

colonnades where rugs and cushioned chairs were arranged; and here in the shade, or, in winter, in the
sun, Moses used to sit and read or play a game of
draughts with a friend. Sometimes he went fishing on
the lake, or sometimes again he would go out duck-
shooting, the sport being to get one's canoe close to the
birds amongst the reeds near the water's edge, and then
to let fly at them with an arrow or a boomerang as they
rose into the air.

There was a certain amount of game up in the
desert, and if the sportsman, with his greyhounds, went
full gallop over the hard gravel and sand in a light
chariot drawn by two swift horses, he might have the
luck to come upon a desert hare, a hyæna, or a few
antelope or gazelle; but it was no easy matter to stand
up in the swaying little vehicle and to take aim with a
bow-and-arrow.

The court was exceptionally gay at that time, and
there was an endless round of parties, at which everybody ate and drank too much. Scantily clothed girls
danced for the amusement of the ladies and gentlemen
who sat about at little tables, dressed in their best and
garlanded with flowers, while the band played cease-
lessly. Other entertainers sang songs, often decidedly im-
proper; and sometimes troupes of jugglers or acrobats gave their performances to the rhythmic sounds
of drums, tambourines, and castanets. Egyptians were
ever a noisy people, and what with their loud voices,

their hilarious laughter, their unrestrained hiccups, and their hand-clapping in time to the music these parties created an astonishing din, which set all the dogs barking outside and kept everybody awake far into the night.

After darkness had fallen the rooms were lit by lamps and candles, some of these lights shining through thin alabaster bowls and vases, arranged to form a scheme for decoration. Garlands of flowers hung from these vases, while others were wreathed around the pillars, the wine-jars and the legs of the chairs and tables. In these garlands and bouquets were lotus flowers, cornflowers, daisies, poppies, roses, lilies, the berries of the woody nightshade, and the leaves of vines, olives, willows, and other trees. Festoons of coloured ribbons adorned the columns; and these, with the rich upholstering of the furniture, the bright hues of the rugs and curtains, and the vivid paintings, made the setting of such parties very brilliant. Elaborate gold and silver plate was used; there were cups and dishes of rich blue faience; and the glass was multi-coloured.

When the court was not relaxed in this manner, etiquette was very much in evidence, and there was a great deal of bowing to the King and to one another, kissing of hands, and touching of foreheads. Rules of precedence and the like had to be strictly maintained, and the exact social standing of each individual had carefully to be recognized. Life at the palace in this respect was an exacting business, and Moses, for one, must have been glad when his military duties took him away from the capital.

Nevertheless, when at length he led the rag-tag Israelites out of Egypt, and exchanged the very elegant and up-to-date conditions in the royal household for the hardships of disorderly desert camps, adopting Hebrew dress, and letting his hair and beard grow, he must sometimes have echoed the bitter complaints of his followers, recorded in the Book of Numbers, when they wailed: "We remember the fish which we did eat in Egypt freely, the cucumbers, and the melons, and the leeks, and the onions, and the garlic; but now our soul is dried away. . . ."

XII

ST. ANTHONY AND THE HERMITS

AMONGST so-called Christian people the idea is very prevalent that this life is a mournful journey through a vale of tears, and that the best thing for a pious man to do is to cut himself off from the world, to mortify the flesh, to pour dust and ashes on his head, and to fill the desert air with his lamentations. This curious belief, for which there is no foundation in the life of Christ, is the outcome of a line of thought to which the human brain has been driven from time to time in every country and every period of history. Life as it is lived is found to be intolerably full of restless ambitions and disappointments, irritations and fears, wants and worries, cares and sorrows; and these are all able to be traced back to the needs, habits, desires, and affections of the body itself. The attempt is therefore made to cut adrift from the concourse of mankind, and violently to mortify the offending flesh.

The fact then becomes apparent that this exhausting asceticism, and the consequent hours of tired-out vacuity, produce an occasional condition of blissful and altogether delightful rapture. This rapture or ecstasy is the great discovery: it is the astonishing secret which is thought to be revealed only to those who have detached themselves from the world and have subdued the body; and the discoverer of it vows that nothing shall induce him to risk the loss of so wonderful a delight by a return to the racket and bustle of social life.

Actually, the teaching of the Founder of the faith was directed towards the proper understanding of the fact that happiness consists not in avoiding the world, but in avoiding servitude to the world; and the ecstatic state attained by the drastic mortification of the body was never advocated any more than was the taking of drugs, which is but another method of seeking a selfish and cowardly escape from the responsibilities of ordinary existence.

The monastic or hermit life was one of the many pagan institutions, quite alien to the original Christian rule, which tacked themselves on to early Christianity. In Egypt, many years before the time of Christ, numerous monks who worshipped the god Serapis were congregated in the desert behind Memphis; and in the same period there were hundreds of Jewish monks, known as the Therapeutæ, who lived on the shores of Lake Mareotis, behind Alexandria, then the Egyptian capital. Both these grim fraternities of anchorites survived into Christian times, and both must have been observed with sympathetic interest by the primitive Egyptian Christians; but the latter did not attempt to emulate them until the end of the third century A.D., the true founder of Christian monasticism being a certain Egyptian named Antonios, now known to us as St. Anthony.

Anthony was born of well-to-do Christian parents about the year A.D. 250, at the little town of Coma, on the west side of the Nile, near Heracleopolis Magna, the modern Ehnasiyeh, just to the south of that part of Egypt known as the Fayûm. This was the year in which the great persecution of the Christians was instituted by the Emperor Decius; and Anthony in his childhood must have seen from time to time, or taken part in, the flight of his co-religionists into the neighbouring deserts. When he was about twenty years of age he developed religious mania and adopted a hermit's life, taking up his abode in one of the disused funerary chapels belonging to the days of Egypt's ancient glory, of which there were many just outside the town. Such chapels are light and airy chambers cut out of the clean white limestone of the sunny hillsides, and I myself have camped in them many a time with much enjoyment; but this fanatical young man was there for no pleasurable purpose. His whole attention was concentrated upon the attainment, through hardship, of the vision of beatitude; and his fight with the flesh took the form of imaginary struggles with animals, women, and other dreadful things, of which we may still read in the stories of his famous Temptations, and at which we, in this age of complexes, are inclined to laugh, though they were no laughing matter for this robust Egyptian youth, whose body was as brawny as his mind was mystic.

About the year 285, when he was some thirty-five years of age, he moved across the Nile to the east bank, and settled himself in a small brick fort which stood disused and in ruins on a hillside in the desert a short distance to the east of the town of Aphroditopolis, the modern Atfih. There was a well near this ruin, beside which a few palm-trees grew; and at first, it seems, he used to emerge from the fort each day to draw water, and to collect the presents of food made to him by his admiring friends. But his reputation for sanctity soon brought too many people to the spot for his liking, and he decided therefore to retire for good into the fort, making arrangements to have the food and water handed to him over the wall.

For twenty years not a soul set eyes upon him; but gradually during this period there grew up around his hiding-place a thriving colony of hermits, some of whom must have fled from the large cities owing to the continued persecutions of Christians under the Emperor Diocletian, while others had come there to carry out in Christian guise the principles of the earlier pagan anchorites, in close proximity to so great and mysterious a saint. Presently pilgrims arrived in swarms from all over the country to have a look at the holy community and to stare in awe at the sun-baked walls of the fort behind which this hidden man of God lived his mystic life; and at length in defiance of Diocletian's edicts, the town of Aphroditopolis became a busy tourist centre; a pilgrim road was constructed, inns and shops grew up beside it, and posting-houses where one could obtain camels and donkeys for hire sprang into existence. The whole thing was like a circus.

Then, in 306 came the news of the accession of the Emperor Constantine, and the cessation of the persecutions; and thereupon the hermits and the pilgrims began to plead with Anthony to come out and show himself. At last he agreed to do so, and the excitement must have been intense when the day came for him to fulfil his promise.

The saint being now over fifty-five years of age, and having endured a twenty years' incarceration, the crowd must have expected a weak and emaciated figure to appear like a ghost from behind the walls; and great was their amazement when a stout, vigorous and perfectly sane man stepped forth into the sunlight, long-haired and long-bearded, but looking to be in the pink of health. They must have been vastly disappointed.

One can imagine Anthony's astonishment, too, when he saw the veritable town which had grown up around his dwelling-place. It was the beginning of Christian monasticism, though little he knew it; and for the next five years converts to this newly adopted method of attaining happiness poured in. Anthony did his best to organize these institutions, but at last the troubles involved became too much for him, and he made a bolt for it into a more remote part of the desert, near the Red Sea, where he lived to be a centenarian.

Meanwhile a large settlement of hermits grew up in the valley of Nitria, now called Wady Natrûn, some forty miles back in the desert behind Alexandria—a desolate spot where a few palm-trees growing beside fresh-water wells were dotted about the banks of salty lakes and salt-marshes. A certain Ammonios, who died in the year 356, was the founder of this settlement: at first he had been there alone, but, as in the case of Anthony, hundreds of hermits had come to live around his hut, the community at length numbering more than six hundred souls, who met together for public worship on Saturdays and Sundays, but otherwise lived in comparative solitude.

Another settlement grew up at the neighbouring oasis of Scete, but here the brethren observed perpetual silence. In the desert near some of the larger cities such as Oxyrrhynchos (Behnesa) and Lycopolis (Assiût) huge communities came into existence; and by the time of St. Jerome there were no less than fifty thousand monks in residence around Tabenna, near the modern Dendereh, a settlement founded by Pachomius about 305. Swarms of them were congregated, too, in the desert hills on the west bank of the Nile opposite Thebes (Luxor), living amidst the ruined temples and tombs of the Pharaonic necropolis.

Many of these hermits vied with one another in the practice of terrible austerities. One man would starve himself for a number of days, and others would then try to beat his record. One would stand upright, supported by a wall or rock, for months together, and others would endeavour to extend the period into years. There were some who shut themselves into little stone huts, where they could never lie down, their food being handed to them through a hole in the wall. Some took up their position on the tops of pillars in ruined temples, where there was barely room to lie curled up at nights, and all day long the merciless sun beat down upon them. The famous Simeon Stylites was one of these, and a whole company of admiring hermits came to dwell around the base of his pillar.

One old monk of Thebes endlessly built huts for newcomers, and when somebody asked him why he thus laboured in the intense heat of the summer sun, he replied: "My body is slaying me; I am determined, therefore, to slay it." Another cried incessantly: "Depart from me, O evil thoughts!" Yet another continually beat his hands against a rock, so that he might learn, he said, like it to feel no pain. The hermit Ammonios being taunted once by some strangers as being an idiot, declared that he had striven for years to attain that very idiocy at which they laughed. A huntsman wandering far out in the desert came upon a hermit nigh starving in absolute solitude, who said to him in reply to the question as to what he was doing: "I, too, am a huntsman; I am hunting for God, yearning to capture Him, so that I may enjoy Him."

It was, indeed, as though a large part of the Egyptian nation had gone mad, for few would admit to-day that this was sane religion; and that it was not true Christianity is now evident from the fact that it was adopted, as I have said, from pagan sources three centuries after the beginning of the Christian era. But mad or sane, these hermits concentrated their entire attention on attaining the longed-for state of bliss; and, believing implicitly that delirious ecstasy, which was really the result of physical exhaustion, was a Christian condition of mind, they fought to reach it by these deadly and terrible battles with the flesh, welcoming the sicknesses and diseases which resulted therefrom, and crying out that God had deserted them if they felt fit and well.

Soon the system spread to Syria and to other countries, where some of the hermits hung themselves in tubs from the branches of trees, and swung there for years at a time; it was adopted in modified and less abnormal form in the west; and at last the monastic rule, under the more reasonable character in which it is now known, became a recognized part of the Christian religion. In Egypt it has survived under fairly easygoing conditions to the present day, and throughout that country there are many little communities of Christian Egyptian monks living in the same places in which these early mystics endured their self-inflicted sufferings.

The bones of Macarius of Alexandria, one of these hermits, who died in about the year 393, still rest in the church of Mâr Makar in Wady Natrûn; the monastery Mâr Antonios still stands near the fort wherein St. Anthony hid himself for those twenty years; and another monastery of the same name marks the place to which he afterwards retired.

XIII

THE INIMITABLE LIVERS

WHEN I hear stories of, or chance to come in contact with, The Bright Young Things of Mayfair, or their more wealthy cousins in New York, I am always reminded of the Inimitable Livers, the *Amimetobioi* as they were called in the Greek tongue, a society founded by Marc Antony and Queen Cleopatra at Alexandria somewhere about the year 40 B.C. The likeness, of course, is not at all complete, for these modern scatter-brains do not attempt so much to live inimitably in respect of their diet as to amuse themselves between meals by whatever means their naughty little minds can devise, whereas the Alexandrian clique tried to do both. Moreover, the Society of Inimitable Livers had two great advantages: the ability to obtain money to spend with even less risk of getting into trouble than there is in modern America, and a public amusement at their excesses which could not now be found in anything like the same degree of obsequiousness either in England or the States.

The great metropolis of Alexandria, which Ferrero calls "the Paris of the ancient world," formed as fair a setting for the pleasures and amusements of these far-

off chasers after the will-o'-the-wisp of happiness as
you could wish for, and it may be entertaining to
steer our magic carpet across the Mediterranean to that
sun-bathed spot, so that we may take a brief look at
the Inimitables at the height of their revels. The city,
purely Greek in character, stood on the sparkling Egyptian sea-coast, behind the island of Pharos, whereon
towered that huge white marble lighthouse which was
regarded as one of the wonders of the world. To the
east of this stupendous construction lay the Great Harbour, and to the west the Harbour of The Happy Return, the two being separated by the Mole or Heptas-
tadium.

Cleopatra's palace covered the breezy Lochias
Promontory on the east side of the Great Harbour, overlooking it and the open sea, and the surge of the break-
ers was ever to be heard in its airy halls. West of it there
were other magnificent buildings also reflected in the
waters of the harbour, including the Forum, the Library,
and the Museum, which was really a huge university.
Behind these rose the Paneum, or Temple of Pan, set
upon a conical mound, and several other temples, of
which the greatest was the Serapeum, dedicated to the
city's god, Serapis. Then there were the Courts of Justice, the Gymnasium, and the Mausoleum of the Kings,
surrounding the magnificent tomb of Alexander the
Great, not to mention the many great houses of the
millionaires.

Running right through the city from east to west was the splendid thoroughfare called the Street of Canopus, a hundred feet wide and three miles long, flanked by buildings and shady colonnades. Other fine streets ran parallel with, or at right angles to, this thoroughfare, the whole town being thus divided into blocks, and having the gridiron formation which is to be seen in New York and other modern cities.

Behind the city was the romantic Lake Mareotis, with its eight islands gay with pleasure-gardens; and at its sides grew plantations of reeds and papyrus, very popular with picnic parties. The Racecourse lay outside the east gate, and near it, down by the bathing beach, were the Gardens of Eleusis, a pleasure-resort where there was an excellent restaurant. The great open-air theatre was near the Forum, close to the Palace; and from its semicircle of marble seats one could look across the stage to Pharos and the blue Mediterranean beyond.

The climate was like that of the Riviera; generally sunny, but sometimes rather cold and rainy in winter, and not intolerably hot in summer, there being an almost continuous northern breeze from the sea. Flowers grew in profusion all the year round; and in spring and early summer the poppies and daisies were a sight. These, with the green palms, the dark cypresses and sycamores, the white rocks, the yellow sand, the many-hued awnings of the houses, and the blue sea and sky, formed a medley of colour which was almost dazzling.

"We are vanquished, mine eyes!" cried Achilles Tatius, the novelist, some generations later, when he saw it all.

The Palace itself was sumptuous. The inner walls were of inlaid marbles, the decorated rafters of the ceilings were covered with gold, and some of the floors were of onyx and alabaster. Tortoise-shell from India, studded with emeralds, adorned the doors; and rich carpets, curtains, and cushions lent vivid colour to the rooms. The furniture was Greek and Roman; and the costumes worn at the court were all made in the Greek style, with the exception of those of some of the old-fashioned Egyptians, and those, again, of the Gallic legionaries who, since 55 B.C., had been stationed here as a support for the Macedonian Household Troops.

The life and soul of the Inimitables, of course, was the dashing little Cleopatra, a pure-blooded Greek, at that time (40 B.C.) a woman of about eight-and-twenty. She was not particularly beautiful, but, as Plutarch says: "familiarity with her had an irresistible charm," and Dion Cassius describes her as "splendid to hear and to see," referring to her fascinating voice, her sparkling wit, and her always *chic* appearance.

She was not at all an immoral character: in fact, compared with many other women of her time, she was decidedly virtuous. There was a serious epidemic of licentiousness in Rome and Alexandria in those days, and, indeed, the professional courtesans were gloomily complaining that their business had been hard hit by the fact that the ladies of fashion asked no payment for exertions of a similar nature.

Cleopatra had been married twice: first to Julius Cæsar—the marriage in this case being valid only according to Egyptian law, and then to Antony; and though her name was linked with those of other men, the gossip could not be substantiated.

She was a harum-scarum little soul in those days, always up to some prank or other; and in many respects Antony, the "colossal child," as Renan calls him, was just the right companion for her. He was a large-sized, easy-going, kind-hearted, swashbuckling fellow, with a neck like a bull's, and muscles like a prizefighter's. He claimed descent from Hercules, and looked like him, except that he was clean-shaven; and, being well aware of the fact, he often used to dress the part. He liked, too, to be regarded as a personification of the jolly Bacchus or Dionysus, and sometimes could be seen, on fête-days and at carnivals, riding in a golden car and being trundled through the streets, accompanied by leaping girls who made a terrible din with their clashing cymbals.

Cicero, who detested him, describes him as a sort of butcher or prizefighter; but actually, in spite of his figure, he was a gentle soul, a brave, silly, vulgar man, having what is called a heart of gold. His soldiers adored him for his frank, generous, and democratic disposition, as well as for his reckless courage; and they liked, too, his sympathetic nature, and the way he used to sob aloud when he visited the dead and dying after a battle.

His first wife, Fulvia, had been a very strong-minded and severe woman, who could not understand him in the least, and was only angry when he bounced out at her to make her say "Oh!" or played some other childish joke upon her. But Cleopatra laughed with him at these pranks, and led him on to others, as, for example, when they used to roam about the city at night in disguise, knock at people's doors, and run away. As an instance of their pleasant fooling, I may mention that once when they were out fishing Antony made a slave dive under the water and fasten fishes to his line, so that everybody exclaimed as he landed them one after the other; but Cleopatra, guessing the trick, caused another servant to descend into the sea and attach smoked herrings to his hook, thereby exposing the fraud amidst general laughter.

We read of a certain occasion on which one of the Inimitables named Plancus dressed up for fun as a sea-god, and pranced about nearly naked and painted blue, having a crown of seaweed on his head and a false fish-tail tied around his waist. On another occasion Cleopatra swallowed a fabulously valuable pearl dissolved in vinegar, in order to bring the cost of one of her dinners up to the impossible figure she had bet her friends she could spend upon a single meal.

The menu of a banquet of the Inimitables makes extraordinary reading. There were sea-hedgehogs, oysters, mussels, and other shellfish, sea-nettles, sea-acorns both black and white, snails, thrushes with asparagus, duck and fowl of many kinds, hare, pork, beef, lamb, venison, boar's head, sow's udder, various vegetables, all kinds of sweets, and a great variety of fruit and nuts.

The whole known world was searched for particular delicacies, and amongst the many dishes served at feasts of this period we hear of peacocks from Samos, grouse from Phrygia, cranes from Melos, kids from Ambracia, tunny-fish from Chalcedon, ass-fish from Pessinus, sturgeon from Rhodes, nuts from Thasos, acorns from Spain, and oysters and scallops from Tarentum. A few years later, I may mention, oysters from Kent and Essex became very popular in Rome, and perhaps in Alexandria, too; and it may be that they were already known to the Inimitables.

Meals were served in the Greek or Roman manner, the guests reclining on couches, while dancing-girls, actors, musicians, acrobats, and so forth, entertained them as at a modern cabaret. Everybody wore wreaths of flowers, and the servants sprinkled them liberally with scents, while the floor was covered inches deep with roses or water-lilies. The wines were potent, and Antony and his friends were usually dead drunk before long; but Cleopatra, it is said, never drank to excess, and remained the one sober person in the room. An Inimitable thought nothing of using jewel-studded gold or silver plate at a banquet, and then presenting the whole lot as souvenirs to his guests; and there is a case on record of a skilful cook receiving the gift of a house and grounds as a reward for a particularly successful meal. Sometimes a chef had to have as many as eight joints of a single kind of meat on the fire at once, each at a different stage of its roasting, so that at whatever hour the erratic Inimitables chose to dine one of these joints would be cooked just to a turn.

The Society maintained its existence for many years; but at length, when Antony and Cleopatra were faced with disaster, its name was changed to *Synapothanou-menoi*, which means "Those who perish together," and with the motto: "Eat, drink and be merry, for to-morrow we die," the last wild banquets were held, and the last pranks played.

XIV

THE ADVENTURES OF SINUHE

IF WE were to find ourselves, after a breathless flight of nearly four thousand years, dropped unobtrusively into the streets of the city of Itht-toui, the luxurious capital of Egypt, in about the year 2050 B.C., we should undoubtedly hear sooner or later the story of the extraordinary adventures of a certain aged member of the Royal Family named Sinuhe; for at that time everybody was talking about him. He had recently come back from foreign parts, and had been loaded with honours by his relative the reigning Pharaoh, himself an old man of some seventy years of age. A very fine house had been specially built and furnished for him by royal command, and, no doubt, we should presently catch a glimpse of him seated on his verandah, sunning his old bones, or pottering around his garden, stick in hand, or we should see him passing down the road in his carrying-chair to take dinner with the Royal Family, or going up into the glaring desert behind the city to have a look at the comfortable sepulchre which was there being constructed for him at the Pharaoh's personal expense.

Anybody who chanced to tell us Sinuhe's strange story would point in the direction of this tomb, and would tell us that therein was to be found the reason why the old man had come back to Egypt after all these years abroad. He had not relished the idea of dying in a foreign country, where the necessary ministrations to his spirit might be neglected; he must always have wanted to be buried in his own land, according to the rites of his own religion; and now that old age had come upon him, the gracious royal offer of a nice tomb for him near the King's own pyramid, had brought him back to the fatherland at top speed.

The beginning of the story takes us back to the last weeks of the lifetime of the reigning Pharaoh's father, who, though of royal blood, had only attained the throne by raising a rebellion and deposing the previous sovereign. Sinuhe, it would seem, was one of the most popular figures in Egyptian society, and since he was perhaps more nearly related to the deposed Pharaoh than he was to the usurper, there was some fear at court that on the latter's imminent death another rebellion might bring the crown back to the rightful line. Sinuhe, however, had no desire to play the leading part in such a disturbance; and he became more and more uneasy as the Pharaoh's increasing ill-health brought the crisis ever nearer.

At length his nerves appear to have gone all to pieces; he thought he was suspected of treason; it seemed to him that the Heir to the Throne, the old usurper's son, was watching him closely; and he was quite sure that the wife of that personage mistrusted him, although, actually, he was devoted to her, and was a great favourite with her children. Now, it happened that the dying Pharaoh was obliged to send a punitive expedition into the western desert to chastise an unruly Bedouin tribe, and the Heir to the Throne was chosen to lead it; but when Sinuhe found that he himself had been given a staff appointment and was to accompany the Prince, his worst fears were confirmed, for he was sure that in the event of the old King's death before the army returned, he would be secretly murdered out there in the wilderness, and reported missing. It would be such an easy and convenient way of getting rid of his popular self.

He managed, however, to conceal his nervousness; but when the expedition, having accomplished its task, was returning, his anxiety increased rather than diminished, for messengers brought news of the imminence of the old Pharaoh's demise, and he was certain that the dreaded event would be the signal for a revolution in which he would be involved. So far there had been no attempt to murder him, it was true; but he was scared at the very thought of what might happen when he got back to the palace. He jumped at the slightest sound.

When they were but a day's march from the capital, and were camped for the night, Sinuhe was aroused from a troubled sleep by the arrival of more messengers who were being conducted to the royal tent which was close to his own; and, springing up in a state of panic, he distinctly heard the Prince's voice raised in lamentation, and knew thereby that the King was dead. Trembling in every limb, he crept out into the night, just in time to see the Prince hurry away into the darkness with some of his most trusted officers, evidently intending to reach the palace and to have himself proclaimed before any opposition could be organized.

The very fact that he, Sinuhe, had not been aroused and told the secret news confirmed his fears that his loyalty was suspected, and he presumed that he would never be allowed to live to see the sunrise. Beside himself with fear, therefore, he hurried through the sleeping camp, evaded the sentries, and dashed away into the desert; nor did he stop running until many miles separated him from the troops. Then, quite exhausted, he lay down to rest until daylight should show him where he was.

At dawn he resumed his flight across the desert, making for the Nile, which ultimately he reached at nightfall, nearly mad with thirst. As soon as it was dark he crept down to the water's edge, and, having drunk his fill, pushed out into the stream in a little boat he had found moored to the bank. Under the stars he floated silently down the river for many miles, and at last landed on the eastern shore, making his way up into the desert which also on this side of the river fringes the cultivated land.

Hiding by day and travelling by night he continued his journey north-eastward for more than a week, skirting the fields, drinking at the wells he happened to pass, and eating whatever he could lay his hands upon. At length he reached the great wall which the late Pharaoh had caused to be built to mark his eastern frontier, and across this he climbed in the darkness, successfully evading the pacing sentries. The vast desert was now before him, stretching away to the borders of Palestine, and here he would certainly have perished of thirst had he not been found, almost at his last gasp, by some Bedouin shepherds, who took him to the sheikh of their tribe.

This man had once lived in Egypt, and, having heard tell of the popular Sinuhe, aided his flight northwards, where at last, after many weeks, he was brought before the Prince of Upper Syria, who also had been in Egypt and who at once recognized him. Soon the fugitive's pleasant manners won him this ruler's affection, and in the end Sinuhe married the Prince's daughter, and was given a beautiful estate, abounding in olive-groves and vineyards, cornfields and orchards.

Here he lived for thirty years or so, and reared a family of sons and daughters. He grew his beard in the Asiatic manner, wore Syrian clothes, and lived the hardy life of a tribal chieftain, in every way different from that which he had been used to in luxurious Egypt. Many adventures befell him, for from time to time he had to lead his men against marauding bands of Bedouin tribesmen; but the exploit of which he was most proud was the successful duel he fought with a famous Syrian chieftain who had fallen foul of him and had vowed to kill him. This fiery personage, a man of immense strength, had the audacity to send him a message one day announcing that he would come over next morning to fight a duel with him, it being the custom in that country to settle family or tribal feuds by single combat under strict rules of chivalry. In parenthesis, I may mention that the famous duel between young David and the tall and hefty Goliath, in the presence of their supporters, is another instance of this custom; but in that particular case David hardly played fair, for while Goliath was spitting on his hands, so to speak, in preparation for the formal duel, David hit him in the eye with a stone when he was not looking.

In Sinuhe's case the duel was fought with perfect correctness. At daybreak, the Syrian marched boldly up the garden walk, accompanied by a crowd of his men; whereupon Sinuhe came out to meet him followed by his entire household, all wringing their hands and predicting disaster. As soon as the combatants were within striking distance of one another, they halted, and at the agreed signal they each flung an armful of javelins at the other. These being successfully dodged, the Syrian rushed forward brandishing his battle-axe, while the Egyptian let fly at him with his bow and arrow, and, to his great joy, hit him right in the throat, so that with a terrible yell the man fell flat upon his face, whereupon Sinuhe finished him off with his own axe, amidst the shrieks and groans of the tribesmen.

The years passed, but one day, when Sinuhe was growing old, messengers arrived, bringing him a letter from the Pharaoh in which His Majesty invited him to come back home, pointing out how very unpleasant it would be to die in a strange land and be buried by foreigners, but promising him a beautiful funeral in Egypt, with a gilded coffin, a handsome hearse, and a band. "And anyhow," the monarch added, "why did you run away? What had you done that anything should be done against you? You had not spoken traitorously; you had not said anything that could be resented, and I had nothing against you."

Sinuhe was so excited when he received this letter that he threw himself on the ground, and poured handfuls of dust upon his head. Then he wrote his reply, in which he explained his flight as being due entirely to an attack of nerves. "It happened like a bad dream," he declared, "as when a man of, say, the Delta suddenly finds himself in the Sudan. There was nothing to be frightened about; nobody had made any accusation against me; yet I was all of a tremble, and my legs ran off with me."

A few days later he bade farewell for ever to his astounded wife and children, and set out for Egypt.

When he arrived at Itht-toui, he was conducted into the presence of the Pharaoh; but now again his nerves gave way, and he fell upon his face, shaking from head to foot, having at last to be helped to his feet by the servants. "My good man, don't behave like this!" the King exclaimed. "Don't stand there entirely speechless."

Then the Queen and the royal family came in, and the Pharaoh said to them: "Look!—this is Sinuhe, who has come back like a son of the Bedouin!" At this the Queen uttered a great cry, for she had once been very fond of him; and her sons and daughters all shouted together in their surprise and pleasure. Presently they hurried him off to the bathroom, for he was very travel-stained, they sent for a barber and shaved off his foreign-looking beard; they combed his hair; they dressed him in new clothes, and threw away his own Syrian garments; they souced him in scent; and they put him to bed in the best bedroom. . . .

Such is his story. Before he died, I may add, he wrote it down, and a copy of the document still survives.

XV

THE QUEEN OF PALMYRA

IN THE great and terrible desert, at a spot about 150 miles north-east of Damascus, and much the same distance due east of the Syrian coast of the Mediterranean, lies the oasis of Tadmur, which marks the half-way point between the sea and the upper Euphrates. Some 1300 feet above sea-level, and encircled by barren hills, it is an area of flat gravel and sand where to-day grows a good deal of parched scrub, but where, in ancient times, a forest of green palms, watered by many wells, delighted the eye of the sun-scorched traveller, as he looked down upon it from the rocky pass through which ran the Damascus caravan-road.

To such a traveller, it must have seemed like a little Paradise, set here alone in the vast and dreary desert, four or five days' perilous journey east of the green uplands of Syria, and that same distance of further hardship and danger west of the fertile Euphrates Valley. Here the east-to-west highway between Mesopotamia and Persia on the one side, and the Mediterranean on the other, met the north-to-south highway between Asia Minor and far-off Arabia; and in very

early times, therefore, a busy caravanserai came into being amidst the shade of the palms, having the name
Tadmor, which is practically the same as that whereby
it is now known.

This caravan-station gradually grew into a great city;
and by the beginning of the third century A.D. the
huge trade between Italy and the Orient, and the re-
current wars waged by the Romans against the
Parthians, had brought the place into such prominence,
and had provided it with such wealth, that it was regarded as the queen of the Near East, being known by a
new name, Palmyra, the City of the Palms. Its riches
may be judged by the fact that in wartime it was
the buffer state between the Roman Empire and Parthia,
each side anxiously soliciting its favour, while in times
of peace it served as the link between Orient and
Occident, the bulk of the commerce between the great
cities and countries of the Mediterranean and the East
passing through its gates, and being heavily taxed by it.

The majority of the population was of Bedouin Arab
race, and though Aramaic was the language used in
official inscriptions and documents, Arabic must have
been largely spoken. The Palmyrans were the most daring caravaneers of their time, and the successful con-
ducting and convoying of enormously valuable mer-
chandise, such as silks, jewels, pearls, and perfumes,
across the desert, was regarded by them as the noblest
service to the state, worthy to be commemorated by

public statues of the great caravan-masters and promi-
nently placed inscriptions recording their names. The
Palmyran horsemen and camel-men were world-re-
nowned; and their archers were so famous that when
the city passed under the nominal control of the
Roman Empire, in the time of the Emperor Severus,
they found employment with the imperial armies in
lands far from their desert home.

In the year 264 the Emperor Gallienus recognized
the importance of Palmyra by giving the title of Governor of the East to Odainath (Odenathus), then ruler
of the city. This Odainath had married a beautiful
Bedouin girl, named Bath-Zabbai, daughter of the
chieftain of the Beni-Samayda tribe, and of his Greek
wife who was directly descended from Antony and
Cleopatra, probably through their grand-daughter
Drusilla, who had married the Roman Governor of
Judaea; and when Odainath was murdered in about
the year 267, this Bath-Zabbai, his widow, became re-
gent of Palmyra on behalf of Wahballath, the eldest
of her three infant sons, who, however, died in 271.

To the Romans the lovely Bath-Zabbai was known
as Zenobia, and soon they were beginning to talk about
her with uneasy admiration. Her city of Palmyra had
grown into a glorious metropolis, and its superb buildings were described with awe by travellers. The principal thoroughfare was in itself a marvel of stateliness and
beauty: for over twelve hundred yards it was bor-

dered on either side by two rows of lofty and beautiful columns, supporting richly ornamented entabla-
tures, roofed across and forming a cool, shady walk. At
intervals along this colonnade of no less than 1500 pillars there were imposing archways leading into other
arcaded streets running at right angles to it.

At one end of this triumphal way stood the vast
temple of Samas or Shamash, the sun-god, over a mile
in circumference, where, in the middle of a paved
court surrounded by nearly 400 columns, 74 feet in
height, stood the holy of holies, having a colonnade
around it of fluted pillars with ornate Corinthian
capitals wrought in bronze. Elsewhere there were other
temples and public buildings; and the palace was a
superb structure, again surrounded by mighty columns.
In fact, the whole city was a very forest of pillars, all
the larger houses and all the public squares being surrounded by these shady colonnades, arcades, and porticoes, so that the interiors of the stone buildings were cool
even in the burning heat of summer.

In this magnificent setting Zenobia lived a life of
the utmost splendour. Trevellius Pollio, the Roman historian, describes her as exquisitely beautiful: her face
divinely expressive, her complexion brown, her eyes
black and flashing, her teeth like pearls, her figure perfect, and her movements graceful beyond imagination.
Upon her head at state ceremonies she wore a sort of
helmet having a band of purple fringed with jewels

around the forehead; and her royal robes were clasped by diamond buckles.

At her court there was the pomp of the Persian Kings, except that her tastes were simple in regard to the number of ladies-in-waiting she employed; but she banqueted in the style of the Emperors of Rome, using gold plate, studded with precious stones. She generally appeared in public on horseback, though sometimes she rode in her golden chariot; and there were times when she would march on foot at the head of her regiments of archers and spearmen, sometimes covering long distances in this manner.

Like a soldier she dined and drank with her officers, who adored her; and she took great delight in supervising personally the training of her armies. She was a great administrator, economical yet splendid, severe when necessary but by nature merciful, always just yet proud and defiant. Besides her own Arabic and Aramaic tongues, she spoke Egyptian perfectly, and a little Latin; and she was scholar enough to write an outline of Oriental history; while her intellectuality is indicated by the fact that she invited to her court, and employed as her chief adviser, the famous Platonic philosopher, Longinus, who had been the pupil at Alexandria of the equally famous Ammonius, and who is the supposed author of the well-known treatise "On the Sublime."

Soon her power had so far extended that Antioch, in

northern Syria, had become her second capital; and
at length she descended upon Egypt at the head of
70,000 men, routed the Roman Army of Occupation,
and in the end was acknowledged Queen at Alexandria,
her descent from the great Cleopatra being recognized.
Thus, when the Emperor Aurelian ascended the throne
of Rome he deemed it best to accept her as his imperial
colleague, placing her head with his upon the Alexandrian coins, and terming her Queen-Empress of the
East.

But the time soon came when he picked a quarrel
with her, invaded her dominions, and laid siege to
Palmyra. For weeks she held out, and when he sent a
letter to her demanding her surrender on easy terms, she
replied defiantly that he must surely be ignorant of the
fact that her ancestress, Cleopatra, died rather than survive her royal dignity.

At last when the privations of the siege began to tell
upon her people, she decided to seek help from beyond
the Euphrates, but since the peril of attempting to
break through the Roman lines was extreme, she insisted upon undertaking the adventure herself.

At dead of night she slipped out of the city, got safely
through the lines, and, mounted on the swiftest camel
she could find, rode hell for leather eastwards across the
terrible desert, dodging the Roman patrols.

Four days' riding, with hardly any rest, brought her
to the bank of the Euphrates, beyond which was safety

and a friendly people; but now a Roman detachment had sighted her, and as she dismounted and ran towards a boat she had seen, her pursuers charged down upon her and she was captured.

She was taken back to Palmyra, which surrendered as soon as the news became known, the philosopher Longinus and some of the chief men of the city being beheaded, but the garrison and inhabitants spared. Thence she was brought to Rome, where Aurelian was accorded a magnificent triumph, in which twenty-eight elephants, two hundred wild animals, eight hundred gladiators, and the tremendous spoils of Palmyra, were features of the procession. Aurelian himself rode in a chariot drawn by four stags, and in front of him walked the beautiful Zenobia, so loaded with jewels and chains of gold that she nearly fainted from fatigue, and had to be supported by slaves.

A few weeks later the Palmyrans revolted, and this time Aurelian showed no mercy. "We spared not the women," he says, "we slaughtered the children, we strangled the old men"; and all the buildings of the beautiful city were wrecked. Some say Zenobia died of grief; but there is another story, that the Emperor gave her an estate near Tivoli, where, with her two surviving sons, she spent the remainder of her days, and such evidence as there is seems to point to the truth of the latter account.

To-day the ruins of Palmyra are amongst the most

impressive and most extensive of all those which have come down to us from the ancient world; and it is only because of the extraordinary isolation of the place that they are not one of the great popular sights in the itinerary of the modern tourist. But we have in England a curiously interesting link with Zenobia's desert city. At South Shields, near Newcastle-upon-Tyne, and at Corbridge, not far distant, the Roman gravestones of an important personage named Barates and his wife, have been found, and from the inscription thereon we learn that he was a citizen of Palmyra who had settled in this part of Britain in the days when the country was a province of the Roman Empire, and that he had married a British lady. It may be that he reared a family on the banks of the Tyne, and in this case there may well be in that neighbourhood to-day men in whose veins runs the blood of the race, or even of the family, to which the great and wonderful Zenobia belonged.

XVI

KING ARTHUR AND HIS ROUND TABLE

THE romances of the Middle Ages and of Victorian times have so completely dressed King Arthur up in mediæval armour, and have surrounded him with such a court of English knights and ladies of the age of chivalry, that it is no easy matter to divest him of these trappings and these surroundings, and to present him to the imagination as Artorius, the British-born but Latin-speaking Roman general of the time of the Emperor Flavius Anastasius, struggling all his life to maintain Britain as a province of the Roman Empire against the advance of the primitive English invaders from across the North Sea. He is, in fact, a Roman-British hero; and his famous battles were fought against the English round about the year A.D. 500, at a time when his oldest compatriots might still have been able to say that in their youth they had seen the Imperial Legions marching seawards to the ships which were to carry them for the last time from the British shores.

The Romans had been in Britain since A.D. 43; and when, between 410 and 440, the Eagles were gradually withdrawn to fight the battles of rival Emperors on the Continent, they left behind them a people who were proud to regard themselves as Roman citizens, and who were soon called upon to defend their province, their Christian faith, and their Roman civilization, against the pagan English invaders.

Things went badly for the defenders, however, and after more than half a century of fighting the whole east coast and part of the south coast, together with its "hinterland," was lost to them. Then came a revival; and a series of successful battles culminated in the great British victory of Mons Badonis (an unidentified place) which completely checked the invasion for nearly fifty years. I may add that our English forefathers began their second advance about 550, and by 580 their conquests had reached, more or less, their final limits.

The traditional hero of Mons Badonis and of that whole campaign which thus held up the invaders was this Artorius or Arthur, and in after years all sorts of legends grew up around his memory, some of which seem to be based on fact, while others appear to have been borrowed or invented. Many of the defeated British migrated to the lands across the Channel, where their name is preserved in the province of Brittany, and thither they carried the tales of Arthur's exploits which ultimately spread through France into Italy. Meanwhile some of the stories were preserved in Britain by Nennius and by the early writers of ballads, and in the first quarter of the twelfth century they were elaborated into a wonderful "history" by Geoffrey of Monmouth.

By this time Arthur had become a sort of celestial figure, whose deeds were recounted with passionate fervour in the west and south of Britain, and whose return to earth as a national saviour was looked for with almost as earnest an expectation as was the Second Coming of Our Lord. He was believed to be alive, sleeping with his knights over the ashes of his last banquet in an underground hall at Caerleon in Monmouthshire: it was said that somebody had once entered this subterranean palace by chance and had seen him there, covered with dust, and that Arthur had opened his eyes for a moment and had asked "Is it time?"

This belief that he would one day reappear when Britain had need of him was so firmly held that in the year 1113 a riot was caused in the church at Bodmin in Cornwall, owing to the fact that a servant attending upon some visiting monks expressed a doubt that the hero was still alive, for which he was promptly knocked down by a native of the place. Until quite recently it used to be said at Tintagel, not far from Bodmin, that Arthur was sometimes to be seen there in the form of a sea-bird, and that one day he would reassume his human form; while at Caerleon it is declared that he was seen in August, 1914, riding with his men at midnight through the neighbouring woods, with lanterns around him and a great crucifix carried before him.

It is impossible to-day to separate history from legend in regard to the story of his life, but I may mention one or two traditions which may have some basis of truth. One of the great historical figures in the wars against the English invaders was Aurelianus Ambrosius, who was an actual or virtual King of western Britain, and was evidently as much a Roman as any other provincial ruler in those days of the break-up of the Empire. There is no question about his historic reality, but tradition credits him with a brother, Uther Pendragon, about whose existence there is considerable doubt.

Geoffrey of Monmouth says that this Uther fell in love with Ygerne, wife of a Prince Gorlois who lived at Tintagel, and, having obtained access to the castle while Gorlois was away, stayed the night with this lady, the birth of Arthur at Tintagel being the sequel to the adventure. The name Artorius was not unknown in the Roman Empire, but is sufficiently uncommon to make one look with interest at that of a certain Artorius Castus, who held a high command in Britain towards the close of the Roman occupation; and it is quite possible that our hero was a scion of the same family, the story about Uther perhaps being introduced later to link him with the famous family to which Ambrosius belonged.

Traditionally Arthur held his court at Caerleon, where he is said very precisely to have celebrated five

Christmases, seven Easters, and one Whitsun; and legend points to a certain mound at Caerleon where his palace was situated, and where he is still supposed to sit sleeping at his table. This mound does actually mark the site of an old Roman ruin, beside which are the remains of the baths of that period; and it may well be that here he resided in the faded magnificence of some old Roman's villa.

A few yards away is the Roman amphitheatre which has recently been excavated, and which was built for the entertainment of the soldiers of the Second Legion, who were stationed here for many generations. They were withdrawn about a hundred years before the time of Arthur, in whose day, therefore, the amphitheatre must have consisted—as the excavations have shown—of an open arena, oval in shape, and surrounded by the sloping embankment on which the soldiers had sat, access to the seats being obtained along handsomely built passages at intervals all round.

Now this site has been called since ancient times Arthur's Round Table, and it may well have been the actual place used by him for his military assemblies and councils, its oval shape being the origin of the stories about his "round table."

As to his battles with the English invaders, which tradition says were twelve in number, there is much to be said for their historic actuality, and any identification of the places named leads to the conclusion that the hero must have led his men far and wide over the whole of western Britain. There is no doubt at all about the battle of Mons Badonis having actually occurred and having been a tremendous victory, for Gildas, writing in 545, speaks of it and of the prolonged check it gave to the invaders who had made no further advance, when he wrote, since their defeat.

The well-known story of the hero's last fight and of his being taken to the Isle of Avalon to die may be based on fact; for Avalon is Glastonbury in Somerset, and there it seems pretty certain that Arthur and his Queen were buried. At any rate in 1177 King Henry the Second was present when graves supposed to be theirs were dug up, and he saw with his own eyes some mighty bones which he had no reason to doubt were Arthur's and a lock of Guinivere's golden hair.

Thus, though the marvellous stories of the King and of the Knights of his Round Table may only here and there have any basis of truth, the hero himself is undoubtedly a real historic figure whose personality and whose exploits were such that men have never wholly forgotten them; but when we make our flight across the ages to his day, we must direct our course not to the knightly period suggested by the later tales, but to that tragic age of the fall of Rome, and we must picture King Arthur dressed as a Roman and vainly endeavouring to maintain the Roman civilization which was crumbling to pieces around him.

XVII

KING BHARTRIHARI ON THE SUBJECT OF LOVE

THE early history of the ancient kingdom of Malwa, in Central India, is very obscure; but there is one ruler of that country whose romantic memory still survives, though the period at which he lived has not been fixed: namely King Bhartrihari, the son and successor of a certain King Gandhavasen. Some scholars believe that his reign is to be dated to the second century A.D., when the Roman Empire, still at the height of its power, was doing a big trade with India; but others place it as late as the eighth century, which would make him more or less contemporaneous with the Emperor Charlemagne in the West and the Caliph Harûn er-Rashîd in the East.

Unfortunately, extremely little is known about Bhartrihari's character or deeds. Tradition says that for the first seven years of his reign, he lived a life of self-indulgent happiness, but that he then made the discovery of the unfaithfulness of his wife, whom he loved to distraction, this so affecting him that he almost entirely renounced the world. In his terrible sorrow he compiled three books, each containing a hundred aphorisms or wise sayings summing up his thoughts on life; and these *Satakas,* or "Hundreds," have come down to us, and have been translated from Sanskrit into English by three or four scholars, the translation which I have here used being mainly that of J. M. Kennedy.

The grief-stricken King places at the beginning of his work a paragraph which provides the clue to his bitter and tragic words which follow. "I believe," he writes, "that one woman was devoted to me; but she is now attracted by another man, while a second woman has designs on me. Curses on them both, and on the god of love, and on the other woman, and on myself!" And, having thus delivered himself, he proceeds to give his views on the subject of love and of women in general, interspersing them between his comments on other matters. From these views one can obtain a fair idea of the effects his unhappy disillusionment had upon him, and by grouping his scattered thoughts as I have here done, his tragic story is revealed with a poignancy which will find, even after all these centuries, a ready sympathy in many romantic male hearts of to-day, though his low opinion of women will be echoed only by the very seriously wounded.

Having been so deceived by his wife, he has many scornful things to say in regard to men's foolishness, and their inability to see through the women they love. Just as a dog will take pleasure in eating the most

decayed bones, he remarks, so a man without discern-
ment takes no heed of the worthlessness of his possessions. Deceived and imposed upon, he compares himself
to a river, falling ever lower and lower, and he pretends
to be glad that there came to him this rude awakening,
for undoubtedly, he says, it is better to roam the mountains with the wild beasts than to live in a Fools'
Paradise.

"True love," he writes, "is the uniting of the hearts
of the two lovers; and when this union is not attained
an embrace resembles merely the contact of corpses."
But most women, being of a flighty disposition, simul-
taneously look at one man, talk to another, and think
of a third, which shows how quite unworthy they are
of men's immaculate love. A woman, indeed, is a kind
of agile snake, darting poison this way and that in her
amorous glances; nor can her victims easily be cured.
"Woe is every man!" he cries, "for he must one day be
pierced by the large, swift voluptuous eye of a woman,
which follows him like a quickly moving serpent, and
finally strikes."

It is well known, he declares in his bitterness, that the
characteristics of women are a sour disposition, a face
hardened by inward vanity, and a nature as difficult to
penetrate as the narrowest mountain pass. Their bosom
covers a heart of stone, their sparkling eyes conceal their
shiftiness, their beautiful lips hide their dishonesty, their
waving hair obscures their insincerity, and their soft

words disguise their cunning. At one moment they can laugh, at another they can weep, and thus, in spite of their deceitfulness, they make men put their trust in them. " 'What a divine expression!' exclaims the man who is blinded by love, being intoxicated with excessive happiness; and yet that woman's wickedness is known to the whole world."

The beautiful features of a woman are praised by the poets, says the King; her face is compared to the shining moon, her lips to the forehead of an elephant; yet her beauty really merits no praise. On the contrary, one should give as little attention as possible to those beautiful creatures, tinkling with jewels, who are only pleasing on account of their looks; for pleasure in their society is but transitory, and love, like life itself, is as unstable as a bubble. "Yet what will not the eyes of a woman accomplish? They will softly and quietly make their way into a man's heart and inspire him with infatuation, with delirium, with dread, and with happiness."

Love, Bhartrihari protests, might well compel even the gods themselves to be the slaves of antelope-eyed women. "Smiles, gestures, modesty, the face half turned away, teasings, jealousies, quarrels, chaff; these are women's tools, with which they forge a chain to bind men around. Eyes downcast, sidelong looks, pretty eyebrows, soft words, shy smiles, artificial motions and attitudes of the body, slow and indolent movements in walking; these things serve women both for ornaments and tools. Indeed, if once our fancy be caught by them, the whole world will seem filled with the sparkling glances of lotus-eyed girls, and with the unsteady feelings displayed in those eyes—those fickle eyes whose magnificence resembles the dark blue water-lily in full bloom."

The face of a beautiful woman, he says, shames the splendour of the moon; her eyes surpass the beauty of the lotus; her complexion outshines the lustre of gold; her thick hair is blacker than the black bee; her bosom makes a man forget the curved forehead of an elephant. Who is there that is not reduced and conquered to abject slavery by the artless and timid glances of lovely women scented with saffron; the melodious tinkling of their loose anklets and girdles; the gentle swing of their pearl necklaces, which rise and fall with their breathing; their softly smiling faces with their frank and innocent looks; and their delicate movements when they walk, like the trembling of the stems of flowers? All the poets were wrong when they called women weak; their power is terrible.

At all seasons of the year they exert their spell. "In the springtime, when the scent of perfume pervades everything, and the air is heavy with the delicious smell of the mango-flowers, and the sweet notes of the birds melt the heart, we feel an irresistible desire for their society. In summertime all things serve to strengthen their power: houses provided with artificial fountains of water, flowers, the light of the moon, fans, pollen dust, the mild and sweet smelling breezes, the shining roofs of the palaces, charming lakes, sandal-powder, rum distilled with molasses, light clothing. And in the rainy season, also, there is much to stimulate love; the brilliant flashes of lightning in the sky, the clouds heavy with rain, the peacocks with their passionate cries, and the soil covered with budding flowers."

"Behold," says the King, "the delicate form of the charming woman who is walking in the moonlight with slow and cautious step, resting now and then in the shade of the trees, and, with her little hand, drawing the veil over her face! Ah, what cannot a clever woman do when she takes possession of a man's heart? She can drive him mad, intoxicate and bewilder him with sympathy and love, mock him, threaten him, please him, and worry him in a thousand different ways. When a woman, inspired by love, sets about some task, even Brahma himself is afraid to place an obstacle in her way! There are men on this earth who can cleave in the brow of a mad elephant, or who can slay a lion; but who amongst the bravest can break the onslaught of love?"

Yet, "women alone are the cause of evil, and there is no other; for the lamp of wisdom and judgment burns in the hearts of men only so long as it is not extinguished by love. A man may preserve his greatness, his nobility, and his learning only until love comes to him; and then a woman opens a way for him to the gates of damnation. She is a whirlpool of uncertainty, a palace of pride, a prison of punishment, a treasury of sin, a fraud in a hundred respects, an obstacle placed before the door of heaven, a field of deceit, a basket of illusion, and the open throat of hell."

A man's peace of mind is destroyed by glances shot from feminine eyes, and he can neither enjoy nor give up the object of his passion. "Indeed," asks the King, "what greater calamity can a man suffer in this world than his own youth, the abiding-place of desire, the cause of dreadful agonies of sorrow, and the ally of the god of love? Fortunate indeed is the man who can retain the mastery of his senses at this critical period of youth, —youth, this waterer of the tree of love, this full moon-tide of women's power!"

But youth passes, and is carried away on the stream of time, becoming at length but a memory. And love is like a flash of lightning in a cloud; and the ardent passion of the woman clasped in her lover's arms will last but a moment. When it is gone, what is there left for a man to do but to seek peace and quiet? There are only two things in this world to which a man should give himself up; one is youth and love, and the other is peace.

As age comes upon us, then, says Bhartrihari, let us liberate ourselves from the delusion of love, for fortunate indeed are those who have freed themselves from

it, as from the poison of a snake. "O my heart, be calm!"
he cries. "When shall I lie at rest on the margin of the
river whose banks of sand shine with a dazzling white-
ness under the moon?—when shall I be able to cry only
'God! God! God!' while the tears flow from my eyes?
My face is no longer youthful, my hair is turning grey,
my limbs are weary, and only love is still strong within
me."

"O Lord, I will meditate upon Thee; I will sit on a
rock in a mountain cave and cultivate a quiet mind; but
when, when shall I be freed from my pain? O love,
when will you leave me? I have striven so hard to acquire knowledge of religion; I have wandered in strange
places; I have freed myself from pride; I have carried
out useless tasks; I have smothered my tears and forced
myself to laugh, though my heart was sad. O love, love,
how much further do you wish to lead me? Away from
me! Away with your side-glances so piercing sweet,
loving and delicate! Cease, cease! I have become a different man; my youth is at an end. Folly is dead in my
heart, and this world is nothing now to me but a handful
of grass."

The agonized voice of Bhartrihari comes to us out of
the remote past of a far country with a curiously
familiar sound, and brings home to us one of the great
lessons which wide historical study has to teach, namely
that we ourselves are not creatures of a limited period
or a single place, but are the reduplications of millions

of human beings of innumerable epochs and lands. All over the face of the historic earth our counterparts have lived, experiencing joys and sorrows perfectly understandable to ourselves. In life's drama or comedy the settings change, but the characters are generally the same.

XVIII

THE LADY WHOM ATHENS DID NOT RECEIVE

IT IS a very significant fact that there is no honourable word in the English language to denote a woman devoid of indelicacy or wantonness, who passes her life as the faithful and loving helpmeet of a man to whom she is not married. The designation "mistress" carries with it the imputation of a carnality which the word "wife" obscures; and the other terms are intentionally offensive. Yet there can be no question that many a woman who finds herself in this invidious position, either by choice or by force of circumstances, has really no more against her than the lack of her marriage-lines. Women, one may say, in their relations with men are divided into the good and the bad; and the good, like the bad, are divided into the received and the ostracized.

But in ancient Athens, the word *hetairai* was employed to denote, without the least reproach, that class of women who in their relationship to men remained always outside the law, and therefore always outside the married ladies' visiting-lists, and yet played an honourable part in the life of the country. They were the women who were not received; yet those who did not receive them were acknowledged to be their moral and intellectual inferiors—a curious paradox which has, however, a simple explanation.

The orthodox Athenian girl was brought up to know as little of the world as possible, to see and hear as little as possible, and to ask as little as possible. It was said by the conventional that the less cause a woman gave to be mentioned by men at all, the better it was for society at large. Her husband was chosen for her by her guardians, and if she were left a widow while still of marriageable age she might be handed on by them to another man together with her money and her chairs and tables.

As a wife she was expected to direct her domestic household, to bear children to her husband, and to give as little trouble as she possibly could. Her boundary, says Menander, ought to be her front door; and though she might sometimes go out shopping, or might make the journey to the house of a friend, her public appearances were reduced to a minimum. In the street it was incorrect for her to speak to a man; the doorkeepers at the theatre were directed to refuse admission to women except when a heavy tragedy was being played; and all banquets were stag-parties. In her own house she could take her meals with her husband only when no male guests were present, and even then she must needs sit upright upon a chair while he lolled upon his couch.

As a result of this seclusion the ordinary lady of a

respectable house was usually a narrow-minded, giggling, uneducated fool of a woman, hardly worth talking to; and her bored husband turned to the *hetairai* for all his intellectual feminine companionship. Plato, following Socrates, tried to show that women had many of the same potentialities as men, and that girls should be educated, and trained in sports, like boys; but this only shocked the hide-bound Athenian matrons, and increased rather than diminished that thoroughly immoral imprisonment of the sex, the hardship of which was so clearly pointed out by Euripides.

Thus the class of accomplished and highly educated women who were beyond the conventional pale, and who were usually recruited from the Ionians of Asia Minor, rose into prominence as a recognized feature of Athenian life, being neither courtesans in our sense of the word, nor marriageable ladies. To distinguish them from the silly creatures men married, they were termed "feminine companions," and they were admitted to be the most brilliant and witty talkers in Athens, as may be read in the thirteenth book of Athenæus. In their lives they boldly vindicated the natural rights of their sex to be regarded as the equals of men in freedom, independence of opinion, and good sense; and they supplied the Athenian males with all that decent and wholesome feminine friendship and intellectual comradeship of which the conventions had totally depleted the family circles.

The paradoxical situation is further emphasized by the fact that the married women, incapable of attracting their husbands by any mental attainments, came to employ in exaggerated degree the trivial arts of coquetry; and at the same time that we hear of their inarticulateness and general stupidity, we read of the powder, paint, and rouge they used even when young, their dyed or false hair, their alluring clothes, and their too high-heeled shoes. The respectable women, in fact, had to rely mainly on those physical charms which their unconventional sisters regarded as merely incidental. The word *hetairai* implies an all-round companionship with the opposite sex, based on an identity of interest; but between husband and wife there could be very little of such understanding, and, indeed, the master of the house was obliged to go out to get the first thing a home might be expected to supply, namely, decent and companionable talk.

As a matter of fact, the trained and habitual freedom of women is always the best deterrent of sensuality in men, and therefore no extraordinary amorousness was expected of these free ladies of the *hetairai* class; whereas the survival of the obsolete segregation of the females in the family circle, with its encouragement in them of prurience and silliness, made the women's apartments in respectable homes the main centres of salacity.

Let us make the acquaintance of the famous and beautiful Aspasia, who is the best example of one of

these honourable women not received by the matrons of
Athens. She was born, probably between 470 and 465
B.C., at Miletus, the Ionian city at the mouth of the
river Maeander; and coming to Athens, she became in
about 445 B.C. the feminine companion of the auto-
cratic ruler and leading citizen of that state, the great
Pericles, a dignified, reserved, and profoundly thoughtful man of middle age who had just divorced his wife
so that she might marry a certain admirer more able
than he to tolerate her stupidity

Pericles was debarred from marriage with Aspasia,
but, defying criticism, he brought her to live in his own
house, where soon she had a *salon* to which came the
greatest men of her time. The stricter married ladies, of
course, cut her, except in the case of certain of them
who, under protest, were made by their husbands to
accompany them to her parties; but Aspasia, sure of the
lasting devotion of Pericles, can hardly have troubled
herself on this account, though she must have been
gratified to find that Pericles entirely gave up visiting
other houses, since she herself was not invited. The
devotion of the two was signal; and it is related, as a
matter for wonder, that he never left the house, or
returned to it, without kissing her.

The great Socrates (born in 469 B.C.) was one of her
constant visitors, and he used to advise his friends to
send their sons to her because of her remarkable intellectual gifts. Xenophon was another of her friends, who,

by the way, sometimes brought his wife with him, much to that lady's indignation, I dare say; and the famous Alcibiades as a young man was yet another frequenter of Aspasia's *salon*. Ictinus, the architect of the Parthenon, used to come, too, with his colleague Callicrates; and Mnesicles, another celebrated architect, was also a frequent guest.

Her two best friends, however, were the philosopher Anaxagoras (born in 500 B.C.) and the sculptor Phidias (born in 490 B.C.), both of whom were much beloved by Pericles; and for many years the four of them maintained an inseparable companionship as happy as it was exalted. At that time Anaxagoras, who preached the doctrine of *nous,* or Mind, as the primal cause, independent of matter, had a great following; but the much younger Socrates, with his rough, untidy clothes, his ugly face, and his strange eyes like a satyr's, had not yet risen to the height of his attainments. Phidias, a baldheaded, hard-working genius, was already famous. The Parthenon sculptures were executed under his direction, and his was the colossal statue of Athena, nearly 40 feet high, which was made of ivory and gold laid over wood; while the greatest of all his works, the Olympian Zeus, dates from the last years of his friendship with Aspasia.

Pericles himself was a big, bearded man of great brain, who is described as sending forth his behests from his huge "gallery of a head." He had been a pupil of Zeno, the Eleatic philosopher, who taught that the nature of God was inconceivable because it was outside all man's limitations of sense and thought; and this free-thinker was another of Aspasia's visitors, as also was Damon, the old musician who had once been Pericles' teacher, but had been banished for a time because of his political views.

One cannot think of the intellectual and artistic giants of the Athens of that amazing epoch without conjuring up a picture of the beautiful Aspasia and this brilliant *salon* of hers, where these men congregated. People said that Pericles consulted her on all matters, and that some of the wars in which he led the Athenian armies were engineered directly by her. She was believed, too, to have helped him in the preparation of those wonderful public speeches of his which were delivered, as the listeners declared, with thunder and lightning in his utterance, and the bolts of Zeus upon his tongue.

In Xenophon's *Memorabilia*, Aspasia is quoted again and again in regard to true love and friendship between man and woman; and she is the chief figure in a work by Æschines the Socratic, wherein her comments on the manners of the women of her day are recorded. She was, indeed, one of the greatest ladies of all time; and much food for thought is supplied by the fact that she was in her lifetime cut by so-called respectable society, and now is usually termed a courtesan.

The day came, however, when Convention, in its usual disguise of Religion, made its inevitable attack upon her and her circle. It seems that certain of the younger and more advanced women of conventional families began to call upon her, and thus, of course, used to meet numbers of men. A charge of impiety was therefore brought against her in about the year 432 B.C. by Hermippus, the playwright, who said that it was against all religion that decent men and women should talk to one another, and that Aspasia's house must really be a place of assignation in the worst sense. Her case was heard in court, and she only escaped imprisonment or death by the frantic eloquence of Pericles, who, almost beside himself with dismay, lost his self-control for once in his life, and pleaded her cause with the tears streaming down his face.

Then they attacked Anaxagoras on some sort of charge of irreligion similar to that which later ended the splendid life of Socrates; and the unfortunate man was hounded from Athens.

The absolute integrity of the noble Pericles himself was next called in question; but he managed to refute the charges. The greatest crime of ignorant and jealous society, however, was committed when their asinine onslaught was directed against Phidias, who was also accused of impiety, and was cast into prison, where he died shortly afterwards, thus bringing to an untimely end his glorious career of service to the higher life.

The love of Aspasia and Pericles survived this wretched attack which had deprived them of their two best friends, and in 429 B.C., when Pericles was dying, he had the satisfaction of receiving official sanction to the calling of his and Aspasia's son by his own name. What happened to Aspasia after his death is unknown, for the story that she formed a union with a certain Lysicles seems to be untrue, since he is known to have died in the same year. Yet though the beginning and the end of her life are obscure, she lives for ever as the gracious influence behind the noblest works of Athens; and her story will always exemplify the broad truth that convention and intellectuality are eternally inimical.

XIX

THE MISADVENTURES OF AN EGYPTIAN ENVOY

IN READING books or documents which have survived
from the ancient world, I have often stopped short at
some ludicrous remark, and have asked myself whether
the writer was intentionally being funny or whether
his absurdity was due to his very lack of a sense
of humour; and in regard to the story which I am about
to relate I must confess that I have no clear idea whether
I am dealing with a sober official report of events or with
a piece of actual comedy. The document in question
appears, on the face of it, to be a record of a series of
actual misadventures suffered by a certain Egyptian
named Wenamon, in about the year 1100 B.C.; and there
seems to be no reason to regard it as other than the
account written by Wenamon himself to his chief, the
High Priest of Amon, on his return from the ill-fated
mission upon which he had been sent.

Wenamon had been ordered by the High Priest to
proceed to the Lebanon to obtain a supply of cedar-
wood from the famous forests, and, by way of credentials, he had been given letters of introduction to

highly placed Egyptian and Syrian personages and also
a small, portable statue of the god Amon, which, it
was expected, would be recognized by them as a symbol
of authority. He carried, moreover, a large sum of
money with which to pay for the timber.

On his arrival at the Egyptian port from which he
was to make the journey by sea to the Syrian coast, he
proudly presented his entire bundle of letters to the
local authorities, who advised him to travel by a certain
Syrian ship which was about to set sail; but Wenamon
was in such a hurry to catch this boat that he quite
forgot to get back these letters, and it was only when
he was far out at sea that he discovered the oversight.
Then, on his arrival at the city of Dor, not far from
Mount Carmel, one of the sailors, believed to be a native
of that place, slipped into the cabin while Wenamon
was admiring the scenery, stole the Egyptian envoy's
money—something like £3000 or $15,000—and bolted
ashore with it. Next morning, therefore, the distracted
victim of these two disasters went straight to the palace
of the ruling prince and cried out to him: "I have been
robbed in your harbour, and, since you are the ruler of
this country, you must be regarded as responsible for the
theft, and must find my money."

To this the prince replied: "With all due respect, let
me point out that if the thief had been living in this
city, and had boarded your ship by stealth, I should
certainly have advanced you the sum while the police

were searching for him; but he belonged to the ship, and all I can do is to search for him."

For nine days Wenamon was kept waiting, but on the tenth day the Syrian skipper set sail; and the envoy was obliged to accompany him, although now he had nothing except the little statue of Amon to obtain him any recognition.

The next important port of call was the city of Sidon; and here the desperate Egyptian carried out a daring coup. With the aid of some of the sailors he entered a shop belonging to a merchant of Dor, over-powered the manager, and stole the cash-box, which contained about £2000 or $10,000, calling out to his gagged and trussed victim: "I will keep this money of yours until you find my money, for it was one of your people who stole it." With that he and his party raced back to the ship, and soon were out at sea once more.

Wenamon hoped to put his case before the Prince of Byblos, the city at the foot of the Lebanon which was his destination, and to obtain his aid; but on the ship's arrival at that harbour he was received with a curt message from that personage saying: "Get out of my harbour!"

Thereat Wenamon sent back a humble note to the prince, who had evidently been informed overland of the theft, asking if he might transfer himself to a certain vessel which was about to sail for Egypt; but to this request he received no reply, and the notice to quit was repeated each morning for the next few days, with the most exasperating regularity. The Egyptian envoy, therefore, secretly made his own arrangements to go aboard this vessel which was bound for the Nile; but when, under cover of darkness, he ventured to land on the quay, he walked straight into the arms of the harbour-master and his police. To his great surprise, however, this official addressed him most politely, saying to him: "The prince desires you to remain here until to-morrow."

At this Wenamon turned savagely upon him, crying: "Are you not the man who has come each day to me saying: 'Get out of my harbour?'—and now you are saying 'Remain here in Byblos!' Evidently your object is to let this ship sail for Egypt without me, so that you may continue to come to me and say: 'Go away!' "

The harbour-master explained that he had orders to detain this other ship until the following day; and the upshot was that Wenamon found himself next morning in the presence of the prince.

The prince, of course, could not at first believe that Wenamon was actually the envoy of the High Priest of Amon, for he had travelled by an ordinary ship, and not by any sort of state vessel, nor had he letters or papers of any kind, and there was also this extraordinary story about his having robbed a merchant of Dor. He therefore told the Egyptian that he would send a messenger to Egypt to find out if his statements were true; and therewith Wenamon had to settle down for some weeks to await the result of this mission.

After a long time the man came back, bringing letters confirming the Egyptian's declarations, and also a handsome present to the prince himself, of 10 little cups made of gold and silver, 500 rolls of paper, 500 coils of rope, 500 ox-hides, 20 linen shirts, 20 measures of lentils, and 5 measures of dried fish. At this the prince at once began the felling of the trees; and in due course Wenamon's delighted eyes saw the full number of logs lying at the water's edge ready for shipment.

At last the day of his departure arrived, and, while he was standing on the beach beside the harbour, looking out to sea, the prince came down to inspect the timber, and, approaching him from behind, tapped him on the shoulder.

"Do not stand there," His Highness said, "thinking about the dangers of your coming voyage. You should rather be thinking about the dangers you are exposed to here at my hands. After all, I have not treated you as some former envoys were treated; they were kept waiting here for seventeen years, and, in fact, they died here. Would you like to see their tombs?"

"No, do not let me see them!" Wenamon exclaimed in anguish, for he had been away from home quite long enough. The prince did not press the matter, but presently returned to the palace, which overlooked the beach, leaving the Egyptian to his own uneasy thoughts. No sooner had he gone, however, than Wenamon observed a fleet of eleven ships rounding a headland close to him, and sailing towards the harbour; and with extreme horror he recognized them as vessels belonging to the city of Dor. Presently somebody on the quay hailed them, asking their business, and Wenamon distinctly heard the reply: "We have come to arrest the Egyptian envoy!"

Thereupon the unfortunate man threw himself upon the sand and burst into tears. One of the prince's secretaries happened to be writing at an open window overlooking the beach, and, seeing the Egyptian's paroxysms, hastened down to him, saying, "Whatever is the matter with you?"

"Can you not see?" Wenamon groaned. "Look at them!" He pointed to the ships. "They have come to arrest me."

The secretary hurried off to the prince, who could think of nothing better to do than to send a servant to the miserable man, carrying a couple of bottles of wine and a mutton chop; but when Wenamon had refused thus to be comforted, he sent another servant off into the town to find a certain Egyptian lady of no reputation who happened to be pursuing her calling at that port, and to tell her to come at once to the palace. Presently she was brought mincing into the prince's presence, much elated at this mark of his favour; and she was at once told to go down to the beach and sing to the unhappy envoy.

Meanwhile the prince interviewed the leader of the men of Dor, and told him that though it would not be correct to arrest the Egyptian while he was on shore, there was no reason why the eleven ships should not pursue him as soon as he set sail for Egypt. As a result of this conversation these ships of Dor moved out of the harbour again, and anchored in the bay; and Wenamon found himself obliged to run the gauntlet. No sooner, however, had he made his dash for the open sea, which, I take it, he did in the darkness of the night, than a great storm arose, and all the ships of both parties were scattered.

The vessel in which Wenamon was carried was driven by the wind right across the open sea to Cyprus, where it was wrecked; and the Egyptian now found himself being dragged, bruised and dripping, towards the nearest town by a very hostile crowd. Fortunately, however, he encountered the princess of these parts driving along the high road, and, observing him, she asked who he was, and gave him her protection.

Here the story breaks off, the remainder of the document having been destroyed, and we do not know what next happened to the sorely tried envoy. But since this appears to be his actual report to the High Priest, it is to be presumed that he came at last safe and sound back to Egypt.

XX

THE HEBREW PATRIARCHS

WHEN an antiquarian discusses the historicity of any ancient Biblical character he generally comes under two fires. On the one hand he is assailed by those who consider it sacrilegious to question the authenticity of the smallest detail mentioned in the Scriptures; and on the other hand he is attacked by the scholars who consider it unscientific to place any reliance at all on any statement made in the Bible not supported by contemporary evidence. For my own part, I feel that since the "historical" matter in the Bible is sometimes useless and sometimes valuable, one must be just as ready to accept or question a Biblical statement as one would be to accept or question a statement made in any other ancient writings. On the one hand intelligent religion does not require any particular belief in the veracity of early Jewish records; and on the other hand Science does not call for wholesale scepticism.

One's first duty is to discount all incidents which may have been borrowed from earlier legends or mythological sources; for instance, the account of Joseph's trouble with Potiphar's wife is so similar to an incident in an ancient Egyptian folk-story known as "The Tale of the Two Brothers," that no great reliance can be placed upon its truth. Next, one has to make allowances for the early writers' belief in the miraculous; and, remembering that precisely the same tests of probability have to be applied to the records of ancient as to those of modern events, one has either to explain away or to discard all abnormal matter.

For example, with regard to the manna which fell from heaven, three or four rational explanations have been put forward, of which the most probable is that the manna was nothing more nor less than one of those occasional snowfalls which occur in Sinai, but which are absolutely unknown in Egypt, and which, consequently, would have come as an immense surprise to anyone who had been resident all his days in the Nile Valley.

Allowance has also to be made for the gradual growth of a story, which is almost inevitable in cases where it has been handed down orally for some generations before being committed to writing: for instance, the story of the Ten Plagues no doubt developed out of an account of various misfortunes which were remembered to have befallen Egypt at about the time of the Exodus, the precise number and specific details being later "padding." This addition of spurious details is often due to the need of filling up gaps in a story, where the facts have been forgotten. For example, the absurd age attributed to Methuselah is probably due to there having

been a number of forgotten generations in the pedi-
gree which had somehow to be covered: actually, of
course, people have lived to about the same age throughout the whole of known history.

With these qualifications it may be said that the
stories of the Biblical patriarchs are apparently historical—surprisingly so, indeed, considering that there is
not a scrap of evidence to show that they were written
down earlier than several centuries after the lifetimes
of the persons described. There is hardly any evidence
to confirm the statements made about the characters in
Genesis and Exodus, but the stories fit in remarkably
well with the known facts.

Let us first consider Abraham. His date is roughly
fixed by the recorded fact that he lived in the time of
Amraphel, King of Shinar, who is to be identified
with Hammurabi, the great Babylonian monarch, who
reigned from 2123 to 2081 B.C. Hammurabi organized
an invasion of the territory in which Ur was situated
in the year 2118 B.C., and this may well have been the
reason why Abraham packed up and left, trekking
across the desert and finally, because of a famine, passing into Egypt; from which country he was told to
depart a few years later.

Now the new chronology which I have put forward
in my *History of the Pharaohs*, and which seems likely
to be accepted as pretty well final, places the accession
of the Pharaoh Amenemhet I in the year 2111 B.C. This

Pharaoh is known to have immediately deported from Egypt the Asiatic foreigners who had settled in the country owing to famine in their own lands; and thus we get a probable date for Abraham's departure from Egypt. He was, in fact, deported as an undesirable alien. Isaac is stated in the Bible to have been born 25 years after Abraham left Ur, and the above tentative dates would thus place his birth at 2093 B.C.

When Abraham came into Egypt (say about 2116 B.C.) his wife was at the height of her beauty according to the story, which means, in the East, that she was then certainly not more than about 20 years of age; and thus she would have been about 25 when they were deported in 2111 B.C. This would make her age about 45 when Isaac was born, which is, in fact, just about the age at which she would have given up all hope of having a child, as the story says. The Bible tells us that she died 37 years after the birth of Isaac, which makes her age 82 at her death—a very likely figure.

I need not pursue the matter further; but the above figures will show that there seems to be a real basis of fact in the Biblical story.

Now let us turn to Joseph. The Bible states that when Isaac was 60 he became the father of Jacob, which, according to the above, would be in 2033 B.C. Jacob had several sons, of whom Joseph was one of the youngest; and, as will presently be seen, Jacob's age at

Joseph's birth may reasonably be regarded as about 44 or 45, the event therefore taking place in 1989 B.C. Joseph was carried off by the slave-raiders when he was 17, that is to say in 1973 B.C., when his father was 61; and he was taken out of prison and appointed to office when he was 30, which would be in 1959 B.C., when Jacob was 74. When Joseph sent for his father, Jacob had mourned his loss for 20 years, according to the Talmud; and this event may therefore be placed at 1953 B.C., when Joseph was 37 and Jacob 80, an age which the Bible makes probable by the statement that he was so old that he had to be carried. Jacob died, according to the Bible, 17 years later, when he must have been 97.

All these figures seem reasonable enough; and we may thus fix Joseph's appointment at 1959 B.C. Now this was the exact year of the accession of Amenemhet III, a Pharaoh who seems to have been so much troubled by famines in the land, due to the lowness of the flood-levels of the Nile, that he had to undertake huge irrigation works: a fact which fits in remarkably with the story of the measures taken by Joseph against the threatened famine. During the course of these irrigation works this Pharaoh constructed a huge canal which still exists, and is to this day called the *Bahr Yusuf,* or "Joseph's Canal," and though, of course, we cannot be certain that the Joseph after whom the canal was named was indeed the Joseph of the Bible, the probability is that this is so.

Thus this Hebrew patriarch appears to have been a perfectly historical figure, and to have held high office under Amenemhet III. The Bible states that the Pharaoh gave him the name Zaphnath-Paaneah. Now Zaphnath is the well-known Egyptian term introducing a second name, and Paaneah is probably a corruption of Paanekh, meaning "the Living," a name which crops up from time to time in Egypt. Thus under the designation "Paanekh," or "Yusuf, surnamed Paanekh," we may one day find some Egyptian record of Joseph which will tell us more about him than we know from the Bible. It is not in the least improbable.

But while the main facts as stated in the Scriptures seem to be correct, the details of the stories, as I have said, are open to question. I pointed out just now that the account of the mess in which Joseph found himself in regard to Potiphar's wife seems to have been borrowed from an Egyptian tale. The following is an abbreviated translation of this story:—

"There were once two brothers, the elder named Anub and the younger Bata; and Anub had a house and a wife, and Bata lived with him, working for him in the fields. One day when they were out at work they ran short of seed, and Anub sent his younger brother back to the house, saying: 'Go and fetch some seed'; and Bata did so, and found his brother's wife seated at home, combing her hair. He said to her 'Get up and fetch me some seed'; to which she replied: 'Get it yourself; I am doing my hair.' He then went to the storehouse and returned carrying a great load of seed, at which she said: 'You are very strong; I have noticed it every day.' And she took hold of him, and said: 'Come, let us take our pleasure and sleep. It will be to your advantage, for I will make you a new suit of clothes.'

"Then the young man became as furious as a lion at this wicked thing which she had said, and she was very frightened. He said to her: 'But you are like a mother to me. Do not say such things to me again.' And he returned to the fields.

"Now the woman, being afraid, took some grease and paint, and made herself appear as though she had been beaten. And when her husband came home he found the house in darkness and his wife lying on the floor groaning. He said to her: 'Who has had words with you?' She replied: 'No one except your brother. When he came to get the seed he said to me: "Come, let us take our pleasure and sleep. Unfasten your hair." I said "Certainly not: I am like a mother to you." Then he was afraid, and beat me so that I would not tell. . . .' "

It is practically the same story, and therefore one is not justified in accepting the incident as historical in connection with Joseph. The Biblical student has to use his discrimination, but, having done so, it is very pleasing to find how much remains which may be called historical in regard to these old patriarchs; not, I hasten to add, that it ought to affect one's Christian faith in the very least if they were proved to be entirely mythical.

XXI

THE REMINISCENCES OF DOCTOR OLYMPUS

A SHORT time ago it was laid down in an English court of law that government officials were not entitled to reveal to the public any statements made to them by persons with whom they had been enabled to converse by virtue of their office. This pronouncement was made, of course, for the purpose of checking in decorous England a certain American habit of journalistic loquaciousness, of which the case then in point was by no means a heinous instance; and though the judge's ruling may enhance the dignity of the present time, it will undoubtedly receive the execrations of those historians of the future who attempt to reconstruct a living tale of our brief to-day.

The writer of history is always better served by the authentic reports of private conversations, and by the narration of events which have taken place behind closed doors, than he is by the account of those which have occurred openly and in the presence of the multitude; and history is poor stuff when it is based only on records of events considered fit for public knowledge by contemporary censors.

History, indeed, to be alive must be condensed biography; and biography derives its real vitality not from its subjects' public acts, nor yet from back-door tittle-tattle, but from just those authentic private revelations of which the most likely source in England has now been closed up by the law.

Take, for example, the case of Olympus, who held the official position of physician to Queen Cleopatra towards the close of her life. Both as an official and as a medical man, he ought, according to this English law, to have held his tongue; but, thank goodness!—he did not do so. He wrote an account of the Queen's misfortunes and published it, relating therein private conversations he had had with her and Antony, describing intimate domestic scenes, and even recording anguished words uttered by her on her sick-bed.

Unfortunately his book is lost, but Plutarch quotes largely from it, and thus its deep interest can be guessed at. Perhaps a copy of it may be found one day in Egypt, where Greek manuscripts, preserved by the dry air, often come to light; or under the lava of Herculaneum, whence already 3000 manuscripts have been recovered, a copy may be waiting to be dug out.

The narrative which Olympus had to tell dealt mainly with the last terrible year of the Queen's reign, namely, from her flight back to Alexandria, her capital, after the defeat of her husband, Antony, at the battle of Actium in Greece, which was fought on September

2nd, 31 B.C., to her death on August 29th, 30 B.C. She was then a woman of thirty-eight years of age—a tragic little figure, her face haggard, and her nerves on edge; and, in spite of her brave and energetic attempts to save something out of the general wreck, there was only despair in her heart.

When she was still a girl, as I remarked in an earlier chapter, she had been married according to Egyptian law to Julius Cæsar, then Dictator of Rome, where, of course, the marriage was not recognized, and by him she had had a child, Cæsarion, now a youth of seventeen, very like his father. Cæsar had intended to make himself Emperor, Cleopatra Empress, and Cæsarion his heir to the new throne; but he had been assassinated before the project could materialize, and Cleopatra, who was then in Rome, had been obliged to return with her baby to Egypt.

That was in 44 B.C., and three years later she had met the rollicking Antony again, whom she had known in Rome. Friendship had ripened into love, and ultimately they had been married, and had had three children —a boy and girl who were twins, and then another boy, who was now three years old. Cleopatra's one absorbing interest was the recognition of her eldest boy, Cæsarion, as the great Dictator's son and heir, and the establishment for him of that imperial throne in Rome at which his father had aimed; and to accomplish this she had encouraged Antony to raise a huge army and to make war upon Octavian, Cæsar's youthful relative who had taken command in Italy.

Now the great clash had come; Octavian had been victorious; and Cleopatra and Antony had fled back to Alexandria, where they were nervously awaiting the coming of their enemy to attempt to give them the *coup de grâce*. Meanwhile, however, Antony had gone to pieces. He had always liked to be regarded as a sort of personification of the jolly Bacchus; but now he was drinking like a fish, and his wife and he, in spite of a deep-seated love for one another, spent half their time in hysterical quarrels.

In the last days of July, 30 B.C., Octavian's army landed on the sweltering Egyptian coast, encamping amongst the palms just outside the city of Alexandria; and thereupon Antony, pulling himself together, led an attack upon the invaders which, in a small way, was so successful, that he came back to the Palace in wild elation, and, all hot and dusty as he was, threw his great arms around the little Queen, and kissed her in front of everybody. Encouraged by this victory he issued orders for a general engagement by land and sea on August 1st; and on the night before the battle he gave a dinner-party at which he and his officers all got drunk, and sobbed together at the thought that on the morrow their faithful slaves might be serving new masters.

Dr. Olympus, I suppose, was there, and it was probably he who related a weird incident which occurred when the guests had gone home, and the city, under the glittering stars, was wrapped in the intense stillness of the hot, windless midnight. In the distance those who were awake in the Palace heard the sound of pipes and cymbals, of pattering feet, and of voices singing a wild and lilting Bacchic song. Nearer came the sounds, as though a tumultuous procession were moving eastwards along the great Street of Canopus; and at length the noise faded away, so that one might have supposed the revellers to have passed out by the eastern gate beyond which Octavian's army was encamped. Yet nothing was to be seen by those who ran to ascertain what it was; and soon the rumour had spread that the ghostly procession was the departure of Bacchus from the doomed Antony and the transference of his patronage to Octavian.

At sunrise Antony marched his men out of the eastern gate, and drew them up in battle formation on the rising ground near the Racecourse, overlooking the enemy's camp; and there he waited to give time for his battleships to move out of the harbour in order to make a simultaneous attack by sea. Then came the final blow; his entire fleet and the main part of his army went over to the enemy; and thereat the wretched man fled back to the Palace, tearing his hair, and shouting for Cleopatra to be brought to him, who, he raved, had betrayed him.

She, the distracted woman, ran for her life to her

mausoleum, a temple-like structure built to receive her body at her death; and therein, with her two ladies-in-waiting, Charmion and Iras, she barricaded herself, bolting the great doors, and piling chairs, altars, and other pieces of furniture against them. There was an upper room in this building, the window of which overlooked the courtyard of the Palace; and in this chamber the three frenzied women huddled, preparing to take their lives.

Presently one of Antony's officers appeared below the window calling to the Queen to come to her raging husband; whereat Charmion and Iras cried out that Cleopatra was about to kill herself, and the man, thinking they had said that she had already done so, ran back to his master with the terrible news.

On hearing it, Antony stood stock still, and all his anger against his wife evaporated. "Now, why delay longer?" he cried. "Fate has taken away the only thing for which I could say that I still wanted to live!" With these words, he hurried to his bedroom, tearing off his armour as he went, and calling to his favourite slave, Eros, to come to him to help him to die. But when Eros came, and realized that he was being asked to drive his sword through Antony's body, he turned the weapon upon himself and fell at his master's feet.

Antony bent down over him and whispered to him as he lost consciousness: "Well done, Eros! Well done!"

Then, taking the sword, he drove it into his own breast, and fell back, writhing, upon his bed. But death would not come, and, as he lay there in agony, another messenger arrived from the mausoleum, saying that Cleopatra still lived; and at this her dying husband insisted upon being carried to her.

Neither the Queen nor her ladies, however, could open the doors of the mausoleum to admit him, for in their frenzy they had driven the bolts deep into their sockets; and therefore the groaning man had to be lifted in through the window, the three women hauling frantically at the ropes which had been fastened to his stretcher, and the men outside standing on ladders and helping as best they could.

Olympus seems to have clambered into the room through the window, but he arrived only in time to hear him gasp those famous words: ". . . I have fallen not ignobly, a Roman by a Roman vanquished," and to see him die in his wife's arms. A few moments later the advance-guard of Octavian's cavalry clattered into the sun-bathed courtyard, and the officer called out to Cleopatra to fear nothing, but to rely on Octavian's clemency. To this she replied that she would surrender on condition that her son Cæsarion was properly treated, for his welfare was always her first thought; and thereat the officer went back to Octavian for further instructions, leaving the Queen to moan over Antony's ghastly body for the rest of the day. But in the late afternoon he returned with a companion, and climbing by a ladder into the upper room while Cleopatra's attention was directed elsewhere, managed to pinion her before she could stab herself with the dagger she had instantly drawn.

That night Octavian entered the city, and having obtained the Queen's promise not to commit suicide, gave her permission to attend Antony's funeral next day. Olympus accompanied her on that sad journey, and he relates how she continuously wept and beat her breast, and how for days afterwards she lay in a high fever, over and over again in her delirium uttering the desolate cry: "I *will not* be exhibited in Octavian's triumph in Rome," and continually begging the doctor to let her die.

It was not till August 28th that she was well enough, though still in bed, to receive Octavian in her room in the mausoleum; but she was very overwrought, and during the interview she jumped out of bed in her nightgown to fetch an old packet of Julius Cæsar's letters to her for Octavian to see. Her secretary was presently called to hand to her visitor a list of her jewels, but this personage having sneakingly disclosed the fact that one piece was not listed, Cleopatra leapt out of bed again, and furiously smacked the man's face and pulled his hair, at which Octavian burst out laughing.

He was glad to find that she had accepted his assurance that he would treat her well and did not seem to have any intention of killing herself; and the same evening he made secret arrangements to have her shipped off to Rome at once with her children by Antony, but to have Cæsar's son, Cæsarion, put to death as a dangerous rival. One of his officers, however, who was sorry for the Queen, told her of these plans; whereat it was as though her heart broke, and she at once made up her mind to die.

Next morning, therefore, she obtained permission to visit Antony's tomb, and, having arrived there, accompanied by Olympus, she flung herself down upon the grave, passionately weeping, and calling her dead husband by name. "O, Antony, Antony," she cried, "if you can do anything for me now, don't allow me to be led in Octavian's triumph; but hide me, bury me here with you—for of all my bitter misfortunes, nothing has been so terrible as this short month I have lived without you."

With that she returned to her rooms in the mausoleum, dressed herself in her royal robes, and then sent a letter to Octavian, asking that she might be buried in Antony's grave.

On receiving this ominous note Octavian despatched an officer running to the mausoleum; but it was too late. Cleopatra was lying dead upon her bed; Iras was just expiring upon the floor; and Charmion, scarce able to stand, was swaying at the bedside, trying to adjust the Queen's crown.

"Charmion!" the officer cried, angrily. "Was this well done of your lady?"

She turned her ashen face to him. "Very well done," she gasped, "and as befitted the descendant of so many Kings"; and with that she fell dead beside the Queen.

Dr. Olympus noted down these brave words in his diary, and afterwards, as I say, published a full account of it all, for which posterity is eternally grateful. Nowadays, it seems, he would merely have been censured and fined for doing so.

XXII

THE FIRST ARMAGEDDON

About fifteen miles south of the later Nazareth, there stood in very ancient times the city of Megiddo, sheltering at the eastern foot of the Ridge of Carmel, some twenty miles back from the coast of the Mediterranean. East of the city lay the Plain of Esdraelon with the Sea of Galilee and the Jordan beyond; and to westwards were these hills of Carmel, with the Plain of Sharon on the farther side, sloping down to the sea. In Biblical times the Plain of Esdraelon became notorious for the many battles fought upon it, amongst which I may mention the victory of Barak over the Canaanites, of Midian over the Gibeonites, of the Philistines over Saul, and of the Egyptians over Josiah; and such fame as a battlefield did the locality acquire that the writer of the Book of Revelations here placed the last great battle of the future, the terrible Armageddon, a name derived from that of this city of Megiddo.

It may be that the sinister reputation of the place was partly due to some surviving memory of the first great battle known to history to have been fought in this area, namely, the victory of Thutmose the Third,

Pharaoh of Egypt, over a confederacy of Syrian states on a date which I fix at April 29th, 1471 B.C. This was one of the decisive battles of the world, and placed Egypt for generations to come as the leading power at the east end of the Mediterranean; but the history of the fight is so little known outside the small group of students of Egyptology that it may be worth while to tell the story in these pages.

Thutmose the Third ascended the throne of the Pharaohs in the year 1493 B.C. as joint sovereign with his step-mother, Queen Hetshepsut; but until that masterful lady's death in 1472 B.C. he was kept very much in the background, and had no opportunity of showing his abilities as a military commander. But no sooner had she "gone west," as the ancient Egyptians used to say, than he leapt out of his seclusion, instantly making preparations to invade Syria, where this very menacing confederacy of kings and princes had come into being, their object being to throw off the loose Egyptian yoke imposed upon them half a century earlier.

Thutmose was at this time a man of about thirty-seven years of age. His height was no more than 5 feet 5 inches, but he was broad-shouldered, strong, and full of nervous energy. He had a big, intelligent-looking head, though rather a low forehead; and his clean-shaven, smallish face was characterized by a great beak of a nose and by a pair of deep-set, dark eyes screened

by bushy eyebrows. The teeth of his upper jaw projected somewhat over those of the lower, and his chin
was insignificant, so that one would not at first sight
have thought him the great man that he ultimately
proved to be; and in this regard I had better say now
that before his death in 1441 B.C. he had led his army
to victory in no less than sixteen campaigns and had
proved himself one of the most brilliant and dashing
generals the world has ever known. His energy and his
reckless personal bravery were alike phenomenal; and
at the same time he was the kindest and most gentle
of men, notorious for the generous manner in which
he pardoned his captured enemies, adored by his coun-
trymen, and reverenced as the ideal Pharaoh for hundreds of years.

The hostile confederacy was under the leadership of
the King of Kadesh, a city on the Orontes, nearly a
hundred miles north of Damascus; and this monarch,
hearing that the Egyptians were about to invade Syria,
had marched his army south to Megiddo, sending mes-
sages to all the Syrian princes and chieftains to meet him
there to discuss their plan of campaign. At the same
time the Pharaoh had advanced northwards across the
desert to Gaza, and along the sea-coast to the city of
Yehem, somewhere in the neighbourhood of the later
Caesarea, and within sight of the Ridge of Carmel.
He had expected to have to march inland from this
point, and to make for Kadesh; but to his surprise he

here received news of the enemy's advance to Megiddo
and of the great meeting of the Syrian princes which
was taking place there.

The representatives of over a hundred cities and states,
he was told, were gathered at Megiddo; but these men,
having come there merely to consult with the King
of Kadesh, had not brought any large bodies of troops
with them, and the enemy's forces consisted mainly of
the army of Kadesh and that of the Principality of
Megiddo itself. But when the news of the proximity of
the Egyptians reached them, it seems that they were
sufficiently confident of victory to remain where they
were, behind the walls of Megiddo, instead of hastening
off, as one might have expected, each to his own city to
gather his men.

There were three roads by which the Egyptians
could cross the hills to Megiddo. The northernmost was
the Zefti Road which mounted the heights behind the
town of Aruna and descended on the other side some
three or four miles north of the city. The middle road
also ran inland from Aruna, but passed through the
hills in a deep and narrow defile which led directly to
Megiddo. The third and southernmost route was the
Damascus road which skirted the Ridge, and led, by a
sharp turn to the left or north, via the town of Taanach
to Megiddo.

The enemy assumed that the Egyptians would advance by this last-named route, which was by far the

easiest and safest; and the King of Kadesh therefore moved his army southwards to Taanach, five miles south of Megiddo, where it was astride the road. The Prince of Megiddo, with the rest of the forces, acting as a second line of defence, took up his position on the open ground a mile or two south of the city; but all the confederate princes remained in Megiddo itself, apparently to watch the battle from its walls. This was on April 27th.

The Pharaoh, however, much to the consternation of his staff, decided to cross the hills by the middle route in spite of the dangers due to its narrowness and to the fact that the troops would have to move almost in single file; and therefore, under cover of the darkness, he pushed forward past the point at which the Damascus road forked off to the right, and camped the night at Aruna, only about eight miles from Megiddo, but separated from it by this defile. He took steps, I suppose, to prevent the news of his whereabouts being carried across the hills by anybody to the enemy; but he could hardly have been sure that his position was unknown, and when, next morning, the 28th, he entered the defile the danger of being ambushed and cut to pieces must have been extreme. Nevertheless, Thutmose insisted upon marching at the head of the line, refusing to allow a single man to go in front of him.

All through the morning the Egyptians threaded their way along the pass, and by 1 p.m. they emerged into the open ground sloping down towards the city, and, by a quick advance, managed to take up their position in a half-circle extending from the north-west to the south-east of Megiddo and touching the brook Kina at either extremity. By so doing the Pharaoh accomplished two objects: he practically hemmed the city in, for the Kina, which was difficult to ford, curved around the back or north of the place; and, at the same time, he cut it off from its defending armies which, as I explained, had moved southwards, expecting his arrival from that direction. He had nothing to fear from the city itself, for it contained only a skeleton garrison, the civil population, and the visiting princes who were now trapped within it; and thus the Egyptian army was able to face southwards and to await on chosen ground the attack of an outwitted enemy trying to cut its way back to its base.

During the afternoon and night the Egyptians rested undisturbed, but early next morning, the 29th, the scouts brought in the news that the enemy was moving along the road towards the city; and when they had come to a point about two miles south-east of Megiddo, the Pharaoh launched his attack upon them from the west, he himself riding in his war-chariot. This attack was completely successful, and soon the enemy was flying headlong eastwards into the Plain of Esdraelon. Here, however, the river Kishon barred the passage of those of the fugitives who could not swim, but since the Egyptian pursuit had left the way to Megiddo open from the east, some of them, including the Prince of Megiddo and the King of Kadesh, were able to dash towards the city, where the garrison, fearing to open the gates, hauled them up over the walls by means of ropes and knotted garments and bed-clothes.

The victory was not at all sanguinary. Only 83 enemy dead were afterwards counted on the field, and no more than 340 men were taken prisoner; in fact, almost the whole defeated army got away and were scattered over the Plain of Esdraelon. They left on the bank of the Kishon, however, a mass of war-material, including 892 chariots, stacks of arms, and much armour, amongst which were the complete suits of bronze and the golden chariots belonging to the Prince of Megiddo and the King of Kadesh. In the camp at Taanach, also, the gorgeous tent of the latter was taken.

Megiddo itself surrendered after a siege of six days; and the total booty was then found to consist, amongst other things, of over 2200 horses, 924 chariots, 200 suits of armour, 500 bows, 2000 head of cattle, 2000 sheep, and 20,000 goats. The hundred and more visiting princes surrendered, and were pardoned and reinstated on condition that each should send his son or other heir to Egypt to be educated; but the King of Kadesh had succeeded in making his escape from the beleaguered city, though what became of him is not known.

Such was the first Armageddon which resulted in the

capture at one blow of nearly every prince of Syria; and though it took place about 3400 years ago, we are able to-day not only to discuss its strategy but, in the Cairo Museum, actually to look at the embalmed body of the victorious commander, Thutmose the Third.

XXIII

SACKCLOTH AND ASHES

IN A previous chapter I pointed out that organized asceticism—that curious group-eccentricity so closely related to suicide—was introduced into Christianity by the mystical Egyptian hermit Antonios, now known as St. Anthony, who died in A.D. 356. The man, however, who first preached the doctrine of sackcloth and ashes to the startled Romans themselves was a certain Eusebius Hieronymus Sophronius, who was born somewhere about A.D. 340 and died in 420, ten years after the capture and plunder of Rome by the Goths—a disaster attributed by many at the time to the enervating effects of these teachings wrongly thought to be Christian.

Hieronymus, as he was generally called, was at first no more of an ascetic than many a poor scholar or artist of this or any other period. He was a strong-minded, self-sufficient, intense character, who did not care two straws about personal comforts or about his appearance, but preferred to go tramping over the world, eagerly to hunt out places of historic interest, or else to sit working amongst his books, forgetting all about dinner or bed, or, I may add, soap and water. He had been educated in Rome, but afterwards lived his frugal, bachelor life in Gaul for some time, residing later in Rome again, and then in Aquileia, in the vicinity of Venice.

He had been brought up in the Christian faith, which was no longer disallowed; and his main interests being theological, we find him presently wandering eastwards to Antioch and the Holy Land, whence, impelled by a sort of misanthropy, he retired into the desert behind Syria, where for four years he lived amongst the hermits who were there practising the ascetic life along the lines laid down by St. Anthony. In this quiet retreat he occupied himself with much content in studying Hebrew, so that he might add a thorough knowledge of its literature to his already wide Greek and Latin scholarship; and incidentally he trained himself in the exercise of austerities even greater than those which were natural to him. Then, at about the age of forty, he returned to Antioch and was ordained as a priest, after which he went to Constantinople, and, in the year 382, came tramping back to Rome, where his learning procured him a position as secretary to the Pope.

He had never tolerated polite society, however, and he seems always to have been peculiarly careless, and —if one may put it bluntly—dirty in his habits, his thoughts having been much too engrossed in his studies to turn themselves easily to matters of personal cleanliness and comfort; and having experienced these peaceful and studious years of unworried and unwashed simplicity in the desert, he had become definitely and violently hostile to the pomps and vanities, his natural distaste for them receiving now the approbation of feverish religious conviction. It was right to be dirty, and to go about in rags, he felt; it was right to starve himself; it was right to be celibate; and with all his passionate heart he hated and denounced the rich, the domesticated, the comfortable, and the clean.

For three years he remained in the scorned metropolis, during which time he completed that great work of translating the Bible into Latin which has immortalized his name. But so remarkable a figure as his could not pass unnoticed in Rome; his piety, his fervour, his scholarship, and his dirtiness, excited interest; and soon he had gathered a following of enthusiastic ladies, all of whom were ready to give up their homes and their wealth at his behest, much to the annoyance of their more practical relatives.

Amongst this group was a rich widow of middle age named Paula, who, with her daughter, was heiress of the great Æmilian family; and when Hieronymus had finished his immortal Vulgate, she and he together conceived the idea of leaving frivolous Rome and going to live at Bethlehem in the Holy Land, where Paula's money should be spent in founding a nunnery and a monastery over which they should rule respectively.

In the year 385, therefore, he set out for the east, and soon was followed by this fervent lady, who joined him at Bethlehem, full of enthusiasm and religious ardour. During the first months after their reunion he took her about the country, introducing her to all the places of sacred interest; and so great was her ecstasy when she was shown the Holy Sepulchre that she threw herself upon the floor of the tomb, licking it passionately with her tongue in her emotional frenzy.

Their building schemes at Bethlehem gradually matured, and at length they found themselves in control of a great settlement peopled by male and female enthusiasts who had left all to follow the new asceticism. Famous throughout Christendom, they were visited by hosts of pilgrims and many dignitaries of the Church; and here they lived out their busy lives until at last Paula died, leaving to her daughter in Rome nothing of her once great fortune, but only a load of debt.

Hieronymus, however, had spent a great part of his time in writing letters and treatises violently denouncing the various heresies which had arisen in the Christian world; and these fulminations from his learned but ferocious pen had brought him so many enemies that at one time, towards the close of his life, he was obliged to fly to the desert for fear of actual attack. He had become, perhaps, a little vain, and certainly very dictatorial; but his besetting sin was this vitriolic method of attack. His words were scathing, and deeply insulting to his opponents; and when at last he died, at about the age of eighty, he was as much hated by some factions as he was beloved and respected by others. His vast correspondence, his many Biblical commentaries, and his scholarly translations, have mostly survived; and under the name of St. Jerome he is now regarded as the most learned and authoritative of the early Fathers of the Church. Yet to-day the clergy do not attempt to disguise their disagreement with his opinions as to Christian conduct; and this fact emboldens me to record here some of those perverted views of his, so that the reader may see how far modern religious thought has shaken itself out of that dark and violent dream wherein the later years of the life of this remarkable man were spent.

Believing that the end of the world was very near, and seeing no reason, therefore, why the human race should not commit suicide by celibacy, he regarded marriage as a disgrace. He wrote to a certain childless widow, who contemplated a second union, asking her how she could possibly think of returning to wedded life "like a dog to its vomit or a washed sow to its mire"; and he expressed his astonishment that she should still wish to have a baby "to slobber upon the parental neck." In order to prevent marriages he said that women should make all haste to spoil their natural good looks by deliberate squalor, so that men should not desire them.

Asked by another lady for advice as to the bringing up of her daughter, he replied, very wisely, that her face should not be rouged and painted, nor her ears pierced; and that she should not be loaded with jewels, nor her hair dyed red like the flames of hell, as was then the fashion. But the rest of his advice is appalling. She should not choose as a companion a girl who was pretty or well-dressed, or who could sing songs; but rather should she make friends with a pale and serious maiden, sombrely attired and having the hue of melancholy. Let her have as her model, he writes, some aged spinster; let her take no part in games; let her hear no music; and let her meals always leave her hungry. "I wholly disapprove of baths for growing girls," he says; "rather, they should blush and feel overcome at the very idea of seeing themselves undressed."

He advises ladies of fashion to have no butlers with curled hair about them, nor fair-haired and pink-faced footmen, nor effeminate actors, nor clean-shaven and well-groomed young men. Over and over again he repeats his fear of song, which indicates his own hardly suppressed love of music. "Repel all minstrels as you would the plague," he says; and he terms them "the devilish singers of poisoned sweetness," adding that "the wanton songs of sweet-voiced girls, which wound the soul through the ears," should be wholly disallowed.

He points out how the lady Paula, after her husband's

death, never sat down at table with any man, and never entered a bath except when she was very ill; how she slept always on the hard floor, her only covering being a rough goat-skin; how she declared that she must make up for her past laughter by weeping, and must disfigure with tears the face which once she had rouged; and how she had said that a clean body and clean clothes imply an unclean soul.

He advises his friends to eat little meat, and to drink little, if any, wine; for, he says: "There is nothing which so inflames the passions as the hiccups." Girls, he declares, should never be allowed to speak to boys, and not so much as to glance at smartly dressed youths with curly hair; and he violently attacks a certain man who wears clean linen, uses toothpowder for his teeth, brushes his hair to the best advantage, and takes frequent baths. He highly praises those holy women who never bathe, who are strangers to all soap, and whose hair is full of little animals.

He repeatedly denounces the Roman ladies whose teeth are clean, and who put rouge and white paint on their faces; and he wittily says: "How can a woman weep for her sins, whose tears lay bare her true complexion by making furrows down her cheeks?" Society women in Rome, he writes, wear robes of shining silk, gold chains around their necks, and pearls from India in their ears; and they scent themselves with musk— all of which is sinful.

These and other letters of his provide us incidentally with some very interesting sidelights on the Rome of his day. For instance, writing in the year 403, he expresses his delight at the decay of paganism. "Every temple in Rome," he states, "is covered with grime and cobwebs, and the Capitol, for all its gilding, is beginning to look dingy. They who were once gods remain under their lonely roofs with horned owls and birds of the night; while the Emperor's robes of purple and his jewelled diadem are decorated with ornaments representing the cross." Yet he loved his fellow-countrymen, and furiously disliked the people of Bethlehem. "If it is permitted to loathe any race," he writes, "I have a strange hatred of the Jews."

He was not a saint, though Rome canonized him as such, but he was a great scholar, and a very doughty champion of his Church; and though we may now smile at his tirades and feel wholesome disgust at his habits, we must always remember that he believed in the imminence of the Last Trump, at which society and all its works should be destroyed. He was only renouncing what he believed certainly to be doomed.

XXIV

THE EXPLOITS OF A NIGGER KING

ONE day, in London, a few years ago, I was called up on the telephone by an American unknown to me, whose soft and cultured Southern voice somehow caused me to picture him as a white-moustached, little old gentleman in a "wide-awake" hat and a black tail-coat. He explained that he was a professor of Ancient History at a university in the States, and he asked for an interview in order to discuss certain archæological matters. I invited him to take tea with me on the following afternoon, and my surprise may be imagined when at the appointed hour an enormous and perfectly black negro was ushered in by the agitated maid. He proved to be a man of considerable scholarship, passionately eager to raise the status of his people, and, with that object in view, anxious to learn how to obtain permission to excavate and makes researches in the Sudan, where he hoped to unearth the buried relics of the ancient glories of his dusky forefathers.

For some time, with shining teeth and rolling eyes, he talked to me about the early history of the negro kingdom of Cush, or Ethiopia, which rose to its highest power in the eighth century B.C.; and he revealed a particular and typical interest in the subject of the ancient religion of his race, especially in its ceremonial and mystical aspect. His enthusiasm was well served by his eloquence; and in highly rhetorical language, which became in the end a trifle too boastful, he invoked a tremendous picture of far-off magnificence, pointing out that, after all, it was fitting that a negro rather than a white man should undertake the study of the remains left behind by that astonishing epoch of nigger dominion.

I do not know whether he has been able to fulfil his purpose or not; but after he had bowed himself out I again read through the grandiloquent and deeply religious annals left by King Piankhi, the most famous of the nigger Kings, and I came to the conclusion that my visitor was probably right in his belief that it takes a negro to understand a negro.

Piankhi came to the throne of Ethiopia in about the year 740 B.C., his capital being the city of Napata, a short distance below the Fourth Cataract of the Nile, about a thousand miles, as the crow flies, south of that river's mouth. To-day you may see there the vast ruins of the place, with its pyramids, temples, and tombs; and amongst these there are the remains of a great temple built by Piankhi, wherein the large inscribed tablet of the King's annals was discovered in 1862.

The life of the court at Napata was an imitation of that of the Egyptian Pharaohs, Egypt being Ethiopia's northern neighbour; and Amon, the great Egyptian god, was the patron deity of the nigger realm, while many other Pharaonic gods were worshipped. At this time Egypt itself had fallen upon evil days, the country being split up into several small kingdoms or principalities; and thus Ethiopia, which was a vast territory commanding a great and well-trained army of black warriors, found itself in a position to invade the northern reaches of the Nile. In some campaign, the details of which are now lost, Piankhi had evidently made his triumphal way right down the river to Thebes (Luxor); and the good behaviour of himself and his troops had caused the Egyptians to regard him almost in the light of a protector from the dangers which threatened them from the north, where Assyria on the east and Libya on the west were hectoring them.

At length, in about the year 722 B.C., messengers arrived at Napata informing the black potentate that a Libyan prince named Tefnakht had overrun all northwestern Egypt; and with this event Piankhi begins his chronicle of victory, opening it with the bombastic words: "Listen to what I did!—I who am a celestially born King, the living image of the sun-god, destined to rule from birth." The story then continues in the third person, the arrival of the messengers being described, and the terrifying tale of Tefnakht's invasion being related, at which, it is said: "His Majesty, with courageous heart, laughed and jested."

"Then His Majesty sent orders to his officers who were commanding his army in Egypt, saying: 'Mobilize quickly; engage the enemy in battle; capture his people, his supplies, and his ships.' And he sent reinforcements into Egypt, saying to them earnestly: 'Do not stop by day or night; do not sit thinking as at a game of chess, but fight at sight. Force battle on the enemy from far off; force it first on the pick of his troops. Harness your war-horses, the best in your stables; draw up your line of battle; for you know that Amon is God, and that it is He who has sent us!' But, he added with great piety, 'When you arrive at Thebes, baptize yourselves in the sacred river, put on clean clothes, and unstring your bows. Do not then boast of your might, for there is no strength to the mighty except in Him, who turneth the weak into the strong. Sprinkle yourselves with holy water at his altars, and bow to the ground before Him, saying: "Show us the way, that we may fight in the shadow of Thy sword." ' "

The expedition thus sent out was fairly successful, but "the heart of His Majesty was not satisfied therewith." Victory after victory was announced, but in each case the phrase is reiterated: "His Majesty was not satisfied"; and at last he cried: "I swear, as God loves me, that I will go north myself!" "Then His Majesty sailed down the river, and, coming forth from the cabin of his ship, mounted his war-chariot, and, raging at his soldiers, cried: 'Is it your duty as soldiers to be slack in my affairs? A great and final blow must be struck at the enemy.' "

Therewith he led his troops to Hermopolis, a city held for Tefnakht by a local king named Namlot, and laid siege to it. Piankhi had brought his *harîm* and many of his female relations with him into Egypt, and after the siege had lasted some time a deputation of ladies from the beleaguered city came to the royal camp, led by Namlot's wife, and, throwing themselves on the ground before Piankhi's black womenfolk, cried: "We come to you, O royal wives, and royal daughters, and royal sisters, and royal concubines, that you may appease the wrath of His Majesty."

On hearing this Piankhi arranged an armistice with Namlot, and addressing him as he lay prone upon the ground, said: "Who has led you astray?—who has led you astray?—who, then, has led you astray that you risked your life by opposing me?" And at the end of this curious repetition of the question, Namlot admitted his crime, and was generously pardoned. Piankhi then entered the city, making his way at once to the temple, where a service was held, after which he went to the palace, where, I am sorry to say, the ladies of Namlot's *harîm* made eyes at him, although his black Majesty "would not even look at them."

Then he asked to be shown the stables; but "when he

saw that the horses had suffered from hunger, he said, 'By God! I swear it grieves me more that these horses have been starved than any other mischief that you, Namlot, have caused.' "

He next marched his army to another city wherein an enemy force was garrisoned, and sent them a message, reading: "You suicidal, silly and miserable creatures!—if an hour passes without your opening your gates to me, you are dead men; and as it would be painful to me to have to kill you, do not close the door upon life, and do not court death in this manner."

Thereupon the garrison at once surrendered, and not one man was killed. Like at the next enemy stronghold he sent in a message, saying: "Open your gates and you shall live; close them and you shall die"; whereupon they immediately surrendered, and Piankhi at once held a service in the local temple.

At length he reached Memphis, the northern capital, where Tefnakht himself was in command; but that personage fled by night on horseback, under the pretext of fetching reinforcements, leaving the garrison to defend the place. Piankhi at once ordered his blacks to take the city by assault, which they did, slaughtering most of the inhabitants, after which he attended divine service in all the most important temples. Next, he crossed the Nile to Heliopolis, where he held another service, washed in the holy pool, bathed his black face in the sacred stream, said his prayers on the holy hill, per-

formed the customary ceremonies in the temple, worshipped at the sacred pyramidion, and finally went alone
into the Holy of Holies, and came out saying that he
had seen God face to face.

After that he went to the city of Athribis, where
again he attended service, and also inspected the horses;
and a few days later he rounded up the miserable Tefnakht, who wrote him a letter, saying: "I can stand up
to you no longer. I am a wretched man, and fear is in
my bones. For days I have not been inside a beer-hall,
nor has any music been played to me; I have gone
hungry and thirsty; sickness is upon me; I have lost
my wig; and my clothes are in rags. Please send a messenger quickly to say you forgive me."

Therefore Piankhi pardoned him, after which, we are
told, the remaining enemy princes came in to submit,
all being kindly received except two of them who belonged to a tribe which ate fish, a thing abhorred by
Piankhi on religious grounds. These two were not allowed to enter the royal presence, but stood trembling
outside until they were pardoned by message and allowed to go.

Then followed another service in the temple, at which
the more or less white choir sang an anthem in praise
of their black conqueror. "O mighty Piankhi!" they
chanted. "Happy is the mother that bore you! She is a
cow, and she has borne a bull!"

The King then returned to Ethiopia with his army

and his ladies; and for many years to come Egypt paid tribute to him and his successors, amongst whom was Tirhakah, who is mentioned in the Bible (2 Kings xix 9), and whose portrait-statue shows him to have been a full-blooded negro, uncommonly like the American professor who came to call upon me.

XXV

HAMMURABI THE INJUDICIOUS

KING HAMMURABI of Babylon, who reigned from
2123 to 2081 B.C., is generally regarded as the greatest
of the early sovereigns of that land; but he is best
known to us by the Code of Laws which bears his name,
although many of the laws contained therein seem to
have been in force for many centuries previous to his
time. This code, containing some 285 laws, is inscribed
upon a block of diorite now to be seen in the Louvre
in Paris, it having been found in 1901 at Susa by
French excavators. At the top a figure of the King is
shown, standing in pious attitude before the sun-god
Shamash, from whom the monarch is supposed to be receiving the code which is written out below.

These laws were held in the highest esteem for centuries after the death of Hammurabi, being called "The
Judgments of Righteousness," and to-day it is the custom
amongst scholars to speak of them in superlative terms
of praise. With this opinion, however, I do not agree. I
think that they indicate an extremely low mentality
in the Babylonians of that age, revealing them as a
benighted people, incomparably lower in the scale of

civilization than the Egyptians of the same period. Indeed, instead of Hammurabi being termed, as he so often is to-day, the Judicious, the Fountain of Law and Justice, he should rather be described as an ignorant, unreasonable and utterly injudicious old savage, the only excuse for whose asinine code is to be found in the general backwardness of his subjects.

The Patriarch Abraham, according to the arguments which I have put forward in my *History of the Pharaohs*, appears to have begun his great trek from the lower Euphrates to Syria and thence into Egypt, at about the date of the accession of Hammurabi to the throne of Babylon; and the conditions which he found on the banks of the Nile must have astonished him. In his new home he would have come under a judicature approximating in humanity and sweet reasonableness to that of recent, if not modern, times; and though he remained to the end of his life something of a savage he must, in his enlightenment, have looked back with horror to the legal pains and penalties imposed upon the wretched people amongst whom he had been brought up.

Let us examine some of these Babylonian laws, and we shall soon see that the conditions they reveal are quite uncivilized. Here, to begin with, is one having reference to the general practice of magic. If a man be accused, says the Code, of putting an embarrassing spell upon another man without apparent cause, the bewitched party shall be requested to jump into a deep part of the river. If, on doing so, he be drowned, then the supposed spell-maker will be seen to have been either justified or innocent; but if he survive the plunge, then the accused shall be thrown in and drowned. Again, there is a law that if one man curse another, and the personage thus accused be proved inoffensive, the curser shall be put to death; but though such a law may have served a good purpose in checking those terrible and formal cursings so upsetting to primitive minds, the injustice will be apparent, since it is obvious that a righteously indignant man would not have a chance if he were to lose his temper with a bland and plausible scoundrel.

Another law says that if, in the case of a trial on a capital charge, a witness give evidence tending to prove the guilt of the accused, but, in the end, the latter be declared innocent, then the said witness shall be executed; which means, of course, that witnesses for the prosecution would always be too scared to come forward. The judge, too, must often have been in a quandary, for if his verdict in a lawsuit should afterwards prove to be wrong, he would be liable for damages, and would forfeit his seat upon the bench.

The law in regard to stolen goods is ludicrous in the extreme. The seller of a stolen article, says the Code, shall be put to death; but should he not be able to be found, then the innocent purchaser must die in his place.

Again, if a man claim an article or piece of property as his, declaring that it had been stolen from him, and if he be not able to prove his ownership, he shall be executed; or if he bring an accusation of theft against another, and fail to provide witnesses, he shall be put to death. A little more reasonable, however, is the law which says that a man who libels another's wife shall be branded on the forehead.

A woman who is unfaithful to her husband shall be drowned or thrown from a high tower, unless he can be induced to forgive her. If she be merely suspected, he may oblige her to jump into the river, her guilt being proved if she be drowned. Any wife who is regarded by her husband as extravagant or neglectful of her household duties is to be drowned; and one who belittles her husband is to be despatched with a like splash and gurgle. If a man cause injury to a woman with child, resulting in a fatal miscarriage, he himself shall not be punished, but his daughter shall be put to death.

If a youth shall have been adopted by foster-parents, but later, having discovered who is his real father, shall return to him, his eyes shall be torn out. A husband may beat a wife; but if a son shall strike his father—in defence of a belaboured mother, for example—his hand shall be cut off. If a man shall strike a superior, he shall receive sixty lashes of the whip.

Wine-sellers, who were usually women, plied a dangerous trade. They were not allowed, under pain of death, to receive money for wine, but only its value in grain; and should a woman supply short measure, she was to be drowned. When criminals came to her saloon, and she did not give information against them, she was to be killed at once on their arrest. If a woman who, by her father's orders, had once served as a priestess should either open a saloon herself or enter somebody else's, she was to be burnt alive.

Any man who destroyed the eye of another man was to have his own eye put out; if he were to break another's leg or arm a similar injury was to be inflicted upon him by the court; or if, in a fight, he should have knocked his adversary's tooth out, one of his own teeth was to be hammered out to teach him manners.

"If a doctor," says another law, "operate on a man, and cause his death, or open an abscess in a man's eye and destroy his sight, the court shall cut off his fingers." This, in an age which knew little of anatomy and nothing of antiseptics, must have meant that there was hardly a surgeon in Babylon with any fingers left at all.

In the time of Hammurabi bricks were coming into fashion for the building of houses, in place of the reeds previously employed; but, the builders not yet being very skilled, walls were liable to fall down. One of the laws therefore says that if the death of a man be caused by a falling wall or by the collapse of a house, the builder shall be executed; or if the son of the owner of a house be killed by an accident of this kind, the builder's son shall be put to death. In the case of a fire the neighbours must have been pretty chary of saving the endangered goods, for the law says that any man deemed to be helping himself to one of the articles is to be thrown into the flames without trial.

A harsh law is one which states that if a woman's husband be captured in battle by the enemy, she shall remain faithful to him, on pain of death, unless he shall have left her unprovided for, in which case she shall be allowed to marry again, being forced, however, to return to her first husband in the event of his escape, any children by her second marriage having to be parted from her. If a wife become a permanent invalid, the husband may take another wife, who shall have an equally legal position; or if she displease him he may get rid of her by saying simply: "I divorce you," or may reduce her to the rank of a concubine. If she protest or say what she may think about him she shall be drowned. If a wife shall have failed to provide her husband with a son, she may give him one of the housemaids as a substitute for herself (as Sarah did to Abraham); but if there still be no offspring, the maid shall be sold into slavery for being so unnatural. If she run away she shall be killed.

Such is the much-vaunted Code of Hammurabi, and though certain of the laws have some sense in them, a great many are as stupid as they are ferocious. Babylon, of course, had not yet risen to the great wealth and importance which later made its name famous; but whatever degree of civilization it may have attained in after years, its inhabitants in 2100 B.C. can only be regarded as a backward people, having an intelligence of very mean capacity. Yet this was the age at which the wonderful civilization of Crete was revealing itself in the building of the palace at Knossos, and at which the cultured Twelfth Dynasty arose in Egypt, with its high ideals and its fastidious life.

Babylon, in fact, was hopelessly behind the times, and its social life at that period was a survival of the prehistoric savagery which many other kingdoms had long outgrown. As the reader will see, I dislike Babylon.

XXVI

PLINY'S COUNTRY HOUSES

I⊤ is not necessary to introduce Caius Plinius Cæcilius
Secundus, or Pliny the Younger as he is now generally
termed. Everybody knows him, for he is perpetually
reincarnated in innumerable shapes and places; and no
public function is complete without him. In England or
America he is usually an M.P. or a Senator; a tidy, careful, well-dressed man, rather pompous, inclined to be
a bore, extremely vain, a pillar of his church, a patron
of the arts, a ready speaker, and a most loyal subject or
citizen. He is always busy, yet he finds time to potter
about his house and garden, giving orders to people; he
reads a number of books, and he dabbles a little, himself,
in literature, being usually engaged in writing his
memoirs, always with an eye to his own lustre.

But in his particular incarnation as a Roman gentleman, born in the year A.D. 61, it may be of interest here
to renew our acquaintance with him, if only it be to
obtain a glimpse of him staying at one or other of his
country houses. He was in the habit of writing polished
and very self-satisfied letters to his friends; and the most

"highly finished" of these, as he calls them, he published in book-form, ten volumes having come down to us. From them an extraordinarily clear picture of the man may be obtained: one sees him patronizing lectures or readings by eminent authors, and noting with deep satisfaction that "almost all the literary people are friends of mine"; going down to a village to lay a foundation-stone, and carefully recording the fact that he did so at his own expense; opening a public library in his native town of Como, and wondering whether his speech had been too ostentatious, seeing that he was speaking of his own munificence; attending a class at the local school, and remarking with satisfaction that the boys became as quiet as mice on his entry; and endlessly making fatuous remarks such as: "I find all wise men agree that one can do nothing better than follow in the footsteps of one's forefathers, provided that they have walked in the right path themselves."

In the year 112 the Emperor Trajan appointed him Governor of Pontus and Bithynia, on the shores of the Black Sea; and after he had held this post for a couple of years or so his letters stop and he vanishes from history, nor do we know whether he met an untimely end, or whether he returned and pottered about on his estate until he was an old man. Some of the letters are of the utmost historical importance: for instance, those in which he describes the eruption of Vesuvius and destruction of Pompeii and Herculaneum; or that haunting message to Trajan in which he asks for advice in dealing with the Christians of Bithynia, stating that he has forced some of them to curse Christ and acknowledge the orthodox gods, and has put two deaconesses to torture in his endeavours to find out the ramifications of this new secret society, but has found nothing more in their ramblings than a debased superstition carried to excessive lengths, and an inflexible obstinacy.

Just now, however, I want only to outline the contents of those letters in which he describes his country houses, for they bridge the gulf of over eighteen hundred years in a quite astonishing manner. The first description is that of his Laurentine villa, on the seashore, about 17 miles from Rome. The front doorway, which was on the east or land side of the house, opened on to an entrance hall, beyond which was a small courtyard in the form of a half-circle, surrounded by a loggia or colonnade having a sloping roof of red tiles and fitted with glass windows. Beyond this was an inner court, also surrounded by a loggia; and on the west or far side was the large dining-room, boldly built on a rocky promontory, its windows on three sides being so close to the sea that on stormy days they were flecked by the spray from the waves breaking on the rocks below. Between the windows there were folding doors, so that in summer the room could be opened up on these three sides; and Pliny adds that, turning from the sea, one could look back through the two courts and through the front hall to the trees and distant hills framed by the open doorway.

From the left or south side of the inner court a doorway led into a large sitting-room, beyond which was a smaller room, looking south. In the angle between these rooms and the dining-room there was a sheltered open space; and on its south side Pliny built a small chamber with a great bow-window overlooking the sea, the inner walls being lined with shelves where he kept a selected part of his library. Next to it was a bedroom in which he could take his siesta, when the sun and the sound of the sea lulled him to sleepiness over his reading.

From the right or north side of the inner court another doorway opened into a large and handsomely decorated room, beyond which was a second room, generally used as a bedroom, commanding a fine view of the sea. Farther to the north were other bedrooms and also the baths, these consisting of a dressing-room, two curved swimming-baths, a washing room, two sweating-rooms, or Turkish baths as we should now call them, and a warm swimming-bath surrounded by glass windows overlooking the sea.

Beyond the baths was the tennis-court, on the far side of which were two tower-like buildings having day-rooms on the ground floor and a small dining-room and some bedrooms above. Eastwards, these rooms overlooked a formal garden surrounded by clipped box-hedges, and backed by the hillside, and near this was a pergola covered with vines. Fig trees and mulberry trees, as well as flowers, grew in this garden, and there was also a large open space, which Pliny calls his exercise ground, sweeping round to the main entrance.

Extending northwards from these buildings beyond the tennis-court there was a covered portico or passage with windows on either side, and between it and the sea was a terrace having long flower-beds in which a profusion of violets grew. At the far end of this terrace and portico there was a suite of rooms looking out on the sea on the west, the terrace and house on the south, and the hills and woods on the north and east; and in one of these chambers, where there was a sofa and some easy-chairs, Pliny used to spend a great deal of his time, especially when people were calling on his wife, or when some noisy festival, such as the Saturnalia, was in progress. Most of the rooms throughout the house were heated in winter by hot air beneath the floors and behind the walls.

The only disadvantage, he says, was the fact that there was no running water, the supply having to be drawn from wells; but, on the other hand, its advantages were many, and it was close to the village where there were some shops, and also three public baths, these being a great convenience when, arriving unexpectedly from Rome, he found the furnaces of his own baths not alight. The views, too, were magnificent, he writes, and the

wooded shores were dotted with charming villas surrounded by beautiful gardens.

In another letter he describes his Tuscan house, at
the foot of the Apennines, north of Perugia. The building, facing south and west, stood on the lower slope of a
hill, with the mountains behind and an open plain in
front, watered by the Tiber. Meadows, jewelled with
flowers, were spread out before his windows, and the hills
behind were covered with olive trees and myrtles. At the
entrance of the estate, some distance from the house,
there was a terrace laid out with beds in different patterns, bounded by trim box-hedges; and beyond this the
drive sloped up between box trees clipped into the form
of birds and animals. A large acanthus tree grew at the
top, and on either side of it were trim walks bordered
by shaped evergreens and shrubs. Beyond was a circular
open space enclosed by a wall hidden behind a mass of
clipped box trees, growing in tiers, and behind this again
was a grassy open space, providing in its natural charm
a pleasing contrast to the artificial beauty of the lower
gardens.

The house faced this meadow-like space, and was
fronted by a large portico, having in the middle what
he calls an old-fashioned entrance hall. At the north end
of this portico the dining-room projected in the form
of a wing, with a large bedroom leading from it, and in
front of this wing there was a marble fish-pond into

which the water fell in a cascade from the high ground beside the house. Near the middle of the portico there was another projection, consisting of rooms surrounding a little courtyard wherein grew four plane trees around a marble fountain, the water from which sprinkled the roots of the trees.

Along the portico were various rooms, and a flight of stairs led to a passage on the upper floor, from the south end of which four rooms opened, one looking out on the front garden, another on the courtyard of the four plane trees, and the two others on the vineyards which came close up to the house on the south side.

Behind the dining-room were the baths, with the usual warm and cold swimming-baths and sweating-rooms, and above this was a large indoor court for ball games, which, I suppose, extended also over the dining-room. At either side of the house on the upper floor level was a loggia or gallery, built above an undercroft, and leading from that on the south side was another dining-room, and also some bedrooms.

Near the vineyards on the south of the house was a riding track passing round a wide, open space, surrounded by plane trees, the trunks of which were covered with ivy, and behind them box trees, dark cypresses, and laurels. Other tracks led off amidst these trees, here and there traversing orchards or open plots of grass where roses grew in profusion, and where there were low clipped box-hedges in ornamental patterns, one

series spelling out Pliny's name and another that of his
head gardener. At the end of a shady avenue there was
a marble temple, wherein stood a stone seat from the
ends of which water fell splashing into marble basins.
Here Pliny used sometimes to dine, and the dishes,
formed in the shape of boats and ducks, used to be
floated in these basins. A small bedchamber led off this
garden-temple, its windows looking out upon the trees
behind, amongst which was another fountain; and indeed, he says, there were so many fountains at different
points along the track that the sound of the tinkling
water was everywhere to be heard.

In these surroundings Pliny lived his contented life,
and when the call came to him to go to far-off Bithynia
he must have said farewell to these country houses and
to Rome with much sorrow; but no doubt he found
compensation in the thought of his coming importance,
and, indeed, his subsequent letters show how happy he
was in his province, laying foundation-stones, inaugurat-
ing public libraries, condemning smelly drains, erecting
aqueducts, extending his patronage to rising young men,
and writing innumerable little letters to the Emperor
and to his friends.

XXVII

THE BEAUTIFUL, ONE-EYED NEFERTITI

THE beautifully executed bust of Queen Nefertiti (or Nofretiti) of Egypt, is now recognized as one of the great works of art surviving from the ancient world. It was found just before the war by a party of German archæologists while excavating the sacred city of Akhetaton, the modern Tell el-Amârna, in Middle Egypt, where the Queen and her extraordinary husband, Akhnaton, once ruled, and it was taken to Berlin, where it is now one of the most cherished possessions of the new museum.

According to the Egyptian law existing at the time of the discovery, everything found during such excavations belonged to the Egyptian Government, but they undertook to give to the excavator roughly one-half of his "finds," and at the end of a season's work all the objects discovered had to be shown to an official of the Cairo Museum, who made the division. The Egyptian Antiquities Department, whose chief is a Frenchman, has recently stated that the head was never shown; but Maspero, Daressy, Brugsch, and other high officials of the Cairo Museum are now dead, and it is possible that one of these allowed it to leave the country, and the Berlin authorities are emphatic that they have documentary evidence that permission for its removal was obtained.

At the time of writing there is thus a dispute as to whether it should be housed in Cairo or Berlin: a fact which prompts me to lead the reader to the court of this sad-faced Queen, and to take a look at her and her family as they were in the year 1354 B.C., that is to say the year of the death of Akhnaton, according to the chronology which I have put forward in my *History of the Pharaohs* (Volume II).

The fair city of Akhetaton was the outcome of the astonishing religious beliefs held by Nefertiti's husband, Akhnaton. In the early years of his reign, while he was still a boy, he had promulgated a doctrine which was in its outward aspect a worship of that invisible and formless Power, named the Aton, made apparent to mankind in the life-giving energy of sunlight, but which, in its inner meaning, was simply a belief in one God, all-powerful, all-loving, the tender Father of every living creature, by whom all things had their being, and to whom cruelty, hatred, warfare, and the like were utterly abhorrent.

Detesting the old priesthoods of Egypt and the multitudinous gods they adored, Akhnaton turned his back on his ancestral capital of Thebes, with its many temples and shrines, and, in the fourth year of his reign, founded this new city at Tell el-Amârna, a short distance back from the Nile on its eastern side; and here on the hard gravel of a flat expanse of the desert, hemmed in by a crescent of stately hills, he laid out his sacred city, planned with wide streets and fine open spaces, at the sides of which stood the many white villas of his loyal subjects who had embraced his faith and had followed him. These houses were set within luxuriant gardens, the flower-beds and groves being formed by cutting trenches and square pits in the gravel and filling them with rich earth brought from the edge of the Nile.

Here he erected a magnificent temple for the Aton, where the beloved sunshine poured down upon flower-laden altars erected in open courtyards surrounded by pillared arcades; and here, too, he constructed a sumptuous palace for himself and the royal family, surrounded by far-reaching gardens, and having artificial lakes whereon floated his gilded pleasure-boats. Life, love, and happiness were the watchwords of his faith; and here amidst all the beauty that Nature and the skill of his artists and craftsmen could provide, he reigned with his Queen for that short period which Josephus calls the "thirteen fatal years."

But happiness was denied to him; and at the date which I have chosen for our meeting with him, he was a sadly emaciated man of hardly thirty years of age, doomed to an early grave, and perhaps subject to occasional epileptic seizures. His swarthy, clean-shaven face, with its pointed chin, was thin and haggard; and in his thoughtful dark eyes below their heavy eyelids there was an expression of weariness which was accentuated by his stooping shoulders and languid gait.

His figure was ungainly, with its lean neck and arms, its poor chest, and its too heavy hips and stomach; and not all his splendid robes, spangled with gold and cunningly sewn with beadwork, could hide his unshapeliness. At the time of our visit he was a sick and sorry man; and the consciousness that his religion was not popular and would die with him cast a settled gloom over his days.

Nor was Nefertiti happy, for it is a trying rôle for any young woman to play who must be the religiously minded wife and companion of a visionary and almost fanatical prophet of a new faith—a man whose piety and good works began in the domestic circle and whose ideal was the largest family of beloved children his spouse could possibly produce. She had been married to him, poor little soul, when she was about ten or eleven years old; her first baby was born when she was thirteen or fourteen; and now, although she was not more than twenty-five years of age, she was the mother of seven children. Indeed, it may be said that the tired look we see in her thin face is that of a weary mother, not strong enough to carry out to this extent the doctrine of the loving fecundity of the sunlight.

Moreover, she had suffered the very common Egyptian misfortune of losing the sight of one of her eyes, over which a cataract had formed. The sculptor to whom she sat for the portrait which is now so famous had been instructed by the King to execute his work always with the greatest realism, and not to hide any defects his patrons might exhibit; and thus he did not shrink from modelling the Queen's blind eye so that it would appear different from the other, and afterwards, in painting the bust, he deliberately blurred the pupil to indicate the greyish film which had grown over the eyeball.

Nefertiti was the daughter (not foster-child as is sometimes said) of a wealthy nobleman named Ay, a gaunt, high-cheekboned man of middle age, very proud of his relationship to the royal family, and always terming himself "King's Father-in-law" as his chief designation. His wife, Nefertiti's stepmother, was a pleasant-faced matron, called Ty, a name also borne by the late Queen Mother, who had been daughter of Prince Yuaa. They had another daughter, Mutnothem, rather younger than her sister Nefertiti, and this princess survived to be the last of the royal family, being married ultimately to the usurper, Harmhabi.

Of the seven daughters of Akhnaton and Nefertiti —there was no son—one had recently died, and her devoted parents had passed through a period of frenzied grief. The fourth girl, moreover, had been as good as lost to them by her marriage to the King of Babylon, for she had gone to her distant home never to return, and news of her was meagre. The eldest daughter, named Merytaton, now a girl of twelve, had recently been married to the prince afterwards called Sakere or Smenkhkere, and at this time, owing to Akhnaton's ill-health, there was talk of making him a partner of the throne, in which case Merytaton would act as Queen, and Nefertiti's position would become little more than that of Queen Mother, a prospect which she did not relish.

The third daughter, Enkhsenpeaton, was now nine years of age, and she had recently been married to Prince Tutenkhaton, now famous as Tutankhamen, a boy of ten or eleven. In the years to come she was to be left a widow at the age of sixteen, and was to make a bid to regain her throne by marrying a prince of the Mittites and making him Pharaoh of Egypt, which was high treason against her old grandfather Ay, who, on the death of Tutankhamen, was elevated to the throne for want of a closer heir.

The other three children were now aged four, three, and two respectively, and were adored by their sick father: so much so, indeed, that the court painters and sculptors were obliged to represent him kissing them, hugging them, and playing with them. In fact they toddle through all the most formal representations of court functions, looking like little goblins, with their shaven heads and their "almond" eyes slanting slightly upwards in the Chinese manner.

Such was the royal family over which Nefertiti watched with that one tired eye of hers; and it was during her brief respites from domestic worries that she sat to the court sculptor who recorded her weariness and her disfigurement so truthfully in stone, yet succeeded in revealing her as still, somehow, a beautiful woman in whose face a certain proud benignity was also expressed.

It is a pity that we cannot stay awhile longer at Akhetaton to scrutinize more closely this strange royal family, and to find out what happened in the end to the Queen. But there is, indeed, an impenetrable veil over the close of her short life. She did not live long, it is certain, for she is not heard of again after the year of her husband's death. Perhaps she died early in the reign of Tutankhamen, and was buried up in the Valley of the Tombs of the Kings, where, maybe, her tomb will one day be discovered.

XXVIII

HOLY BONES

THE great success of Christian Science is mainly due to the fact that it offers a means of curing the sick, and its rapid spread seems to have reminded orthodox Christians that one of the Church's most popular functions in early times was the performance of miraculous cures, that is to say cures effected by the appeal to the sick person's faith. In the case of the Roman Catholic Church the recent stimulation of this part of religious life was no difficult matter, for the ancient custom of preserving holy relics and of employing them as tangible aids to faith had never died out; but the reformed Churches were handicapped by the fact that the use of holy bones and other revered objects for this purpose is forbidden.

I am not going to offer an opinion here as to whether the employment of relics believed to be miracle-working is canonical or not, or—what is much more important to the lay mind—whether it serves a purpose sufficiently salutary to the body to outweigh its deleterious effects upon the intelligence. I want only to say something about the origin of the practice, and then to make the journey into the early centuries of English history so as to see the thing at work.

In the beginning, I suppose, the custom had something to do with the widespread prehistoric belief that a man's virtue resided in his flesh and bones, and hence that the absorbing of that virtue might be effected by contact with them. Primitive people used to eat the flesh of a dead hero or drink his blood so that his strength might pass into them, or they used to carry a piece of him about with them, which led to the custom amongst South American Indians and others of shrinking a human head until its size was so small that it could be worn as an ornament. In Ireland, for example, there was a practice which persisted into the Middle Ages of picking out the brains of a dead enemy, mixing them with clay, and rolling them into a ball which could be carried in the hand. King Connor of Ulster once had his head cracked open by one of these balls thrown at him by an enemy.

In Ancient Egypt the embalming of the dead had nothing to do with this train of thought, for the bodies were hidden away in tombs and were not exposed as relics; but there are certain traces of a primitive custom of handing on virtue by drying and preserving the placenta, and also by placing a dead ruler's skin upon the shoulders of his successor, this latter practice seeming to be the origin of the belief which still survives in the phrase about Elijah's mantle falling upon Elisha's shoulders. I do not think that the bones of Joseph were carried up out of Egypt by the Israelites for any purpose of this kind, but simply so that the body should not be left in a detested land; yet we read in the Bible that in the eighth century B.C. somebody was cured by touching the bones of Elisha, which shows that the virtue of holy bones was already believed in.

In the Buddhist religion, which was already going strong many generations before the time of Christ, the use of relics for the cure of sickness was very prevalent. Buddha's teeth are preserved in many places, though in Ceylon the famous tooth, which is of very ancient date, is actually a piece of ivory about the size of one's little finger. Mohammedans also make use of relics, but this, of course, does not carry us back to a period as early as that in which the custom appears in Christendom.

The early Christian Fathers make many references to the use of relics: St. Ambrose (A.D. 340–397), for example, tells of a man recovering his sight by touching the bones of two martyrs; and St. Jerome (A.D. 345–420) denounces a certain Vigilantius who had scoffed at their efficacy. In fact, so widespread did the custom become that in the seventh century it was decreed at the Trullan Council that all altars which had no holy relics upon them should be destroyed.

In England the early Irish missionaries who carried Christianity to Northumberland in 635 A.D. evidently brought the custom with them, for they were soon digging up the bones of the sainted dead and using them as miracle-working relics; and at the same time the missionaries from Rome were introducing the practice, and towards the close of that century we find Benedict Biscop coming back to England from Italy with a whole collection of bones. The skeleton of St. Cuthbert, who died in Northumberland in 687, was dug up and became a famous miracle-worker; and when the monks of his monastery on Holy Island fled before the Danish Vikings they carried the bones about with them during centuries of wanderings, finally placing them at Durham, where they still rest.

They also took with them the skull of St. Oswald, King of Northumbria, who had been killed in battle in 642. Oswald's body had been buried on the spot where he fell, but his enemies exposed his severed head and right hand on a post; and later the head was taken to the monastery, and it is now at Durham. The right hand was sent to Bamburgh Castle, where it was preserved in a silver casket and wrought great wonders; but later a monk of Peterborough stole it and took it to that place. Meanwhile the rest of the body had been dug up, and one arm and shoulder found its way to Glastonbury, while the left hand is now preserved, I believe, at Soleure in Switzerland. The trunk of the body went to Bardney in Lincolnshire, and in the tenth century it was transferred to Gloucester, where ultimately it was lost.

Glastonbury had a most extraordinary collection of relics, including the bones of two English saints and those of a Pope, bits of the above-mentioned Benedict Biscop and Abbess Hilda of Whitby, and some of the supposed bones of St. John the Baptist. Pershore Abbey in Worcestershire possessed a very efficacious piece of the skull and some of the ribs of St. Ædburga, granddaughter of Alfred the Great, preserved in a golden reliquary. Evesham Abbey in the same county had the bones of St. Credan, a former Abbot, and St. Wistan, an English prince murdered in 850.

At Bury St. Edmunds the bones of St. Edmund, the King of East Anglia, who was killed by the Danes in 870, were preserved in a wonderful jewel-studded shrine; and amongst the jumble of other holy relics belonging to the same abbey I may mention some of St. Edmund's nail-parings, and the coals over which St. Lawrence was roasted in about the year 258; while, in the Middle Ages, Thomas à Becket's boots were added to the collection and worked wonders.

At Selby Abbey in Yorkshire was preserved in the highest honour a finger from the hand of St. Germanus, the famous Bishop of Auxerre who lived in the fifth century: it had been stolen from the monastery of Auxerre by a monk named Benedict, who founded the house of Selby. At Chester the chief relic was the skeleton of St. Werburgh, a royal lady who had died in Staffordshire in 699, and had been dug up nine years later; and at Ely were the bones of her aunt, St. Etheldrida or Audrey, who had died in 678 and had been dug

up by her sister, St. Sexburga, in 695. Sexburga's bones
were dug up in their turn by her surviving sister, St.
Ermenilda, mother of the above-mentioned Werburgh;
and the remains of all these four ladies were instrumental
in effecting hundreds of cures.

At Rochester the bones of the seventh century St.
Paulinus were preserved in a silver casket; and at St.
Albans the supposed bones of St. Alban, martyred in
the year 303, were dug up and placed in a shrine by
King Offa in 793, although there is some reason to
suppose that Alban was really buried at Caerleon in
Monmouthshire.

Every abbey, cathedral, and large church, in fact,
had its relics to which increasing respect was paid, until
at the time of the Reformation the country was dotted
all over with places to which pilgrimages were made and
at which miracles were performed; and the ultimate
revulsion of feeling against the whole thing may best
be seen in a letter written in 1539 by Dr. London to the
Lords Commissioners at the dissolution of the monas-
teries. After listing the relics in the abbey at Coventry,
which included the arm-bone of St. Augustine of Hippo
—a great miracle-worker, this,—he writes with wither-
ing scorn: "Your lordships shall also find here a piece of
the most holy jawbone of the ass that killed Abel."

The Venerable Bede, writing in the eighth century,
tells many stories of the miracles wrought by the relics
of St. Cuthbert. There was a man, for example, who

had lost the use of his legs, so the monks took the funeral shoes from Cuthbert's dead body and placed them on the invalid's feet, and in a few hours he was cured. A boy who suffered from fits was cured by placing in his mouth some of the mud left at the spot where Cuthbert's corpse had been washed; a man whose face was deformed by a huge swelling was restored to health by rubbing the place with a piece of calf's skin once used by the saint; and another boy who had a sore eye was cured by the application of some hairs from the dead saint's head.

These miracles were real enough: they were simply faith-cures such as are performed all over the world to this day by one means or another; but the interest of what I have been saying lies in the fact that these emotional experiences took place in sedate England. It is so astonishing to think of our own forefathers digging up decomposed dead bodies and loading the altars of churches still in existence with these extremely unpleasant holy bones.

XXIX

THE DISASTER AT HERCULANEUM

GENERAL interest has recently been aroused by the recommencing of the excavation of the city of Herculaneum, which was destroyed in the year A.D. 79 during the short reign of the Emperor Titus. Previous work on the site has led to the discovery of several buildings and many objects; and thus, since there is already sufficient material at hand by which to reconstruct some of the main features of the place, we may choose it as the goal of one of these flights into the alluring realms of Antiquity.

It was situated at the foot of the beautiful vineyards and orchards which sloped steeply up to the crater of Vesuvius; and as it was placed almost exactly at the middle point of the fair coast of the Gulf of Naples, half-way between Neapolis (Naples) and Pompeii, it commanded a superb view of the hills of Surrentum (Sorrento) and Capreae (Capri) on the one hand, and those of Puteoli (Pozzuoli) and Pithecusa (Ischia) on the other. Away to the right was Misenum (Miseno), where, in the time of Augustus, a huge naval harbour had been constructed, and to the left, beyond Pompeii, stood Stabiae (Castellammare), a flourishing little town; but Herculaneum considered itself superior to any of these, and it could certainly boast of having some very important and cultured citizens, including members of the Imperial Family.

There was, for example, the gentleman who lived in the Villa Suburbana, and who was a follower of the philosophy of Epicurus. In his library of 3000 scrolls there were many rare words, including some of the writings of that master and many of those of Philodemus; while his collection of bronze and marble replicas of Greek busts and statues was famous. Here the Sleeping Faunus, the Drunken Silenus, the Reposing Hermes, and many other celebrated works of art were to be seen; and there was a whole gallery of the busts of the philosophers, amongst which was that of the unfortunate Seneca, who, a few years previously, had ended his life with his head in an oven, at the special request of Nero.

The owner of this villa, however, was only one of many intellectual personages who had gathered here partly because of the beauty of the Campanian country, and partly because the climate was much better than that of northern Italy, the air being tempered by cool sea breezes in summer and being rarely sharp in winter. Moreover, the journey to Rome by the well-kept Via Appia was easy of accomplishment, the metropolis being not more than 120 miles distant as the crow flies;

and the sea voyage, coasting along close to the shore all the way, was not more than 130 miles.

The sunny little town itself, too, was so very pleasant, and so well laid out. The main street, over 30 feet wide, had sidewalks paved with inlaid marbles, and the shops were excellent. Many statues, revealing the irreproachable artistic taste of the municipality, were to be seen; and there were ornamental fountains by the dozen. Pompeii was not in the same class.

The open-air theatre was a magnificent structure, having sixteen or eighteen tiers of stone seats forming a wide crescent facing the orchestra and the stage. At least three thousand people could be accommodated; and here again there were scores of first-rate statues. The Basilica, a sort of Town Hall or Assembly Rooms, was also a very fine building; the Forum left nothing to be desired, and the Public Baths were most comfortable.

The gardens of several of the private villas were famous for their beauty, and the owners of some of these houses were very proud also of the elegant paintings which adorned their walls, executed by the best artists in the land. One such painting, representing a large-eyed and beautiful girl, perhaps the Muse of Poetry, just about to write, and sucking her pen thoughtfully, was very highly spoken of.

The streets of the town sloped right down to the sea, and the bathing in summer was popular. Naval officers used to be rowed over in swift galleys from Misenum, which was some 15 miles away, and after the morning swim, followed by a sun bath, they would have their midday meal with their friends and go on perhaps to an afternoon performance at the theatre, returning to the fleet after night had fallen.

The corpulent and asthmatic old Admiral, Pliny (the Elder), was wont to come over in this manner, usually to pay his respects to a lady named Rectina, the wife of a certain Tascus, who had a villa just outside Herculaneum; and sometimes he would go on to visit his friend Pomponianus, whose house was at Stabiae, beyond Pompeii. The whole bay, in fact, was dotted with villas and towns, and the sheltered sea was busy with ships, some belonging to the naval docks at Misenum, others entering or leaving Puteoli, which was the main port of the trade with the East, and yet others plying between the different towns—all of which shipping could be seen from the windows of Herculaneum.

The great disaster occurred in the early autumn of the year 79, and we may hear the story from the lips of the younger Pliny, nephew of the Admiral, who at the time was living with his mother in his uncle's house at Misenum. An extraordinary cloud like a huge pine tree, he says, was observed above Vesuvius, and the Admiral, whose hobby was the study of natural phenomena, at once ordered a galley to be manned so that he could go closer to observe it.

He was just stepping on board when he received a

note from his lady friend, Rectina, begging him to come to her, as she was frightened; and at this he boldly gave orders to his skipper to head straight for Herculaneum and Vesuvius, towards which a strong wind was blowing. As he drew near to the shore, however, cinders began to fall on the deck, and he was implored by his men to abandon his mission.

"Never!" he exclaimed. "Fortune favours the brave!" But at the next deluge of ashes he ordered the skipper to turn and steer for Stabiae, which was then in little danger. Rectina would have to shift for herself, but he might attempt the rescue of Pomponianus.

On arrival there he found that personage busy packing his valuables, but as there seemed no immediate cause for fear, and as the wind might be expected to drop at nightfall, thereby enabling them the more easily to push off from the shore again, he went into his friend's house and enjoyed a good dinner. Maybe he drank too much wine, but at any rate he fell off to sleep thereafter, and, as his nephew says, snored loudly.

He awoke to find himself thick in ashes and the walls rocking with earthquake shocks. Running out of the house into the pitch darkness, he and Pomponianus tied cushions on their heads to protect themselves from the falling cinders; and accompanied by men carrying lanterns and torches, they hurried down to the beach. But here, to their horror, they found the wind and sea too high to permit of the galley being launched; and therewith the Admiral sat down on the sand, panting, and cursing himself for not making his escape earlier.

Then came more earthquakes, and Pomponianus, wild with fear, rushed off into the darkness and was never heard of again. Gradually others of the party took to flight, and at last Pliny was left with only two slaves. He tried, with their aid, to rise, but could not do so; for, what with his asthma and the poisonous fumes in the air, he was struggling for breath. Then they, too, ran away, and the old Admiral fell back unconscious upon the sand.

Meanwhile his nephew at Misenum had spent the night with his mother and the other members of the household in the courtyard of their house, for fear of the walls falling upon them; but when morning came, bringing hardly any light, and the earthquake shocks increased in violence, they decided to leave the town. A crowd of people followed them into the open country, where there was no danger to be feared from collapsing masonry; but while they waited there a huge black cloud came rolling towards them from Vesuvius, and before they had time to continue their flight for more than a mile or so it descended upon them, enveloping them, as the younger Pliny says, in darkness as black and dense as that of pent-up places which have never seen the light. From all around came the screams of women and children, and the frenzied shouting of men; for everybody thought that the end of the world had come, and, indeed, our informant says that the only reason why he did not start screaming himself was that he believed all mankind was perishing together, a thought which he found very consoling.

At last the light came back, and the sun was seen like a dull red ball in the murky sky. The whole landscape was transformed, everything being covered with a deep layer of ashes; but now the earthquake shocks had ceased, and the people, themselves grey with volcanic dust, began to venture back to Misenum, where the damage was found to be not very extensive.

There was still, however, a dark haze over the neighbourhood of Vesuvius, and it was not till the third day that a search party was able to venture forth to look for the Admiral. They found him lying dead upon the beach, just where he had been left by his slaves. Stabiae and the villages round about were half wrecked and were grey with ashes; Pompeii had mostly disappeared, buried under the cinders; but a more terrible fate had overtaken Herculaneum. A stream of molten lava had poured right over it, and not a trace of it was to be seen.

XXX

PRINCE PTAH–HOTPE LOOKS AT LIFE

SOME 4570 years ago there ascended the throne of Egypt a studious young man called Isesi, who, as Pharaoh, assumed the name Dad-Ke-Re, which means "The Permanence of the Spirit of the Sun." He took this name, it seems, because his studies in antiquity had brought him to the highly satisfactory conclusion that he was directly descended from the Sun, which had once manifested itself on earth as a King of Egypt and had founded the dynasty of the Hawks, whose blood ran in Isesi's veins.

As a consequence of this discovery he gave himself the title Si-Re; "Son of the Sun," which ever afterwards was the proudest designation of the Pharaohs; and, to show to the world this permanence of the solar line, he caused a grand table of the annals of his royal ancestors to be inscribed upon stone, recording in brief the events of every one of the years back to the time of the first Pharaoh, Meni, nearly eight centuries before his own day, and the names of the kings before Meni who had reigned as successors of the Sun. It seems, too, that he

spent much time in the Record Office with his Keeper
of the Royal Archives, studying the history of his
country and the genealogy of his house.

Now, there lived in Memphis a certain aged Prince
Ptah-hotpe, who, I think, must have been his uncle, and
who had held the positions of Judge of the High Court,
Minister of Education, Minister of Public Works,
Chancellor of the Exchequer, Privy Councillor, and
Prime Minister. He was a very clever old fellow, well
versed in all the recorded sayings of the wise men of the
Past, and whose own smart remarks were quite worthy
to be remembered; and it was only natural, therefore,
that the scholar Pharaoh should ask him to make a little
book of these, so that, as he said, the Royal mind might
be instructed in "the wisdom of olden times."

The Prince, as a matter of fact, had been thinking of
doing this, and of giving the book the form of a collection of maxims addressed to his son; and now, therefore, he penned the following letter to the Pharaoh:

"O King, my lord," he wrote, "grey hairs have come
upon me, old age is advancing, and the years of my
decline have arrived. Decrepitude has taken the place
of freshness, and some new defect descends upon me
every day. My eyesight is failing, my ears are stopped,
my vigour is diminished, my brain is dull, my mouth is
dumb and speaks not, my mind forgets and cannot even
recall the events of yesterday. Every bone in my body
aches, pleasure is turned to discomfort, and the flavour

of everything is vanished. . . ." He then went on to ask to be allowed to retire from office, promising to spend his time on preparing the proposed book, which should "instruct the unlearned in knowledge of the world and also in the rules of polite discourse." .

The Pharaoh, of course, gave his consent, and Prince Ptah-hotpe retired into private life. Old age for him, I dare say, was not so bad as he had painted it: he had a charming house, with broad verandahs where he could sit and warm his bones in the sun; he had a beautiful garden, full of flowers and fruit trees planted around a lotus pool; there were plenty of servants to wait upon him; and his sons and grandchildren often came to visit him. Moreover, he always had the entertaining diversion, denied to us of the present day, of preparing a comfortable abode for his spirit to dwell in after his body had died.

The handsome building which he was erecting for this purpose stood on the high ground of the desert, a short distance back from the city, not far from the pyramid which was being constructed for King Isesi. It consisted of a courtyard and portico, four rooms and some passages, as well as the actual chamber wherein his body was to rest. The walls of these rooms were covered with painted and sculptured representations of the things needful for his spirit's well-being, and of the servants and others who would make their ghostly ministrations to him; and there were scenes illustrating the ordinary affairs of daily life in which he was likely to be interested.

The building still exists, and many years ago I helped to dig it out of the sand. On some of the walls there are rows of figures of handsome young men and healthy-looking young women from the Prince's estates, bringing all manner of good things for his spirit's enjoyment: bread, cakes, vegetables, fruit, oxen, young calves, gazelles, geese, wine, beer, and so forth.

Elsewhere there are scenes representing the gathering of the corn on his lands, the trapping of wild duck in the marshes, the cutting up of immense quantities of meat by a whole army of butchers, and several other pleasant pictures, amongst which the Prince himself is many times shown, wearing a variety of wigs, different sorts of collars, a white linen kilt with a starched front, and sometimes across his naked breast the broad ribbon of the Order of Scripture Readers, of which he was Grand Master. Here, too, you may see his son, for whom he wrote his book of maxims: he is carrying a combined pen-case and inkpot, and two of his pens are stuck behind his ear, while he hands to his father's ghost the list of farm produce which he had just written. In another picture he has just wrung a goose's neck in the presence of the paternal spirit.

In the meantime, while the old gentleman was amusing himself thus in preparing his future home, he did not neglect the making of his promised book, which,

when it was finished, proved to be so popular that copies
were made of it for hundreds of years, and ultimately it
became a standard book in the schools. Here are a few
wise sayings from it which are still applicable at the
present day, in spite of the passage of nearly forty-six
centuries since they were composed:

"If you wish to maintain a lasting friendship in the
house at which you are in the habit of visiting, try to
avoid talking to the ladies. There are thousands of men
who have gone after these beautiful creatures, and have
been ruined by them, being deluded by their soft bodies;
but they have turned into things that are harder than
rock. The pleasure is only for a little moment, and it
passes like a dream."

"Do not go into a beer tavern, for it is unpleasant to
hear words reported as having come from your mouth
when you do not remember that you said them. And
then again, if you fall down you may break your bones,
but nobody will come to your help. Even your drunken
friends will get to their feet and say, 'Throw out that
drunkard!'"

"Do not be arrogant because of your knowledge.
Listen to what is said by the uneducated as well as by the
cultured, for the limits of art can never be reached, and
no artist is in full possession of his skill. Words worth
listening to are as hard to find as precious stones, and
yet they may be found amongst mere slave-girls in the
kitchen."

"Do not try to scare people, for it effects nothing. What God has decreed happens."

"If you are a man of small position and are in the service of a man of high standing, remember nothing of his former insignificance, and do not exercise your mind in regard to what you know about his past. Respect him on account of what has happened to him, for wealth does not come of itself."

"It is God alone who raises the status of a person who climbs into favour: it is not effected by a man's elbow."

The old Prince ends his book with a piece of advice which will never be out of date. "When Death comes, it seizes the baby which is at its mother's breast as well as him who has become an old man. When, therefore, that messenger comes to you to carry you away, let him find you—*ready*."

Human mentality has not changed much since Ptah-hotpe sat writing on his verandah in ancient Memphis. We have advanced sufficiently since 2645 B.C. to smile at Isesi's claim to solar descent, and to disbelieve that a goose would be of much use to the Prince's spirit; but that is all. Modernity has whittled down our creeds, but it has left our conduct as it always was—in urgent need of "the wisdom of olden times." It is surprising to think that that need was felt already nearly forty-six centuries ago—an age which is pretty well as long before the reign of Tutankhamen, for instance, as the fall of the ancient Roman Empire is before our own times. It shows how deeply, when he thinks of it at all, man resents and always has resented the oblivion of death: it is the triumph of memory, with all its romance, its drama, its comedy, and its sheer experience, that he wants to assure.

After all, we are not mere leaves of a tree that we should fall to the ground and be trodden into dust, leaving nothing behind. We are intelligent entities, thinking constructive thoughts and doing conscious deeds, building up, on the whole and little by little, that human race of the future which is to establish a new earth and a new heaven; and vastly can we profit by the experiences of our predecessors, both by their achievements and their failures, their wisdom and their stupidity, if only we will turn about sometimes, as Ptah-hotpe did, and make the mental journey into that vast region of the Past which lies there, open and alluring and full of entertainment.